ENGLISH

RE★ENGLISH START

ADVANCED 1

NEWRUN

PREFACE

40개국 이상에서 출판! 세계가 인정한 학습서가 왔다

성경 다음으로 가장 많이 팔린 이 책은 1945년 출간된 뒤 40개국 이상에서 출판된 베스트셀러이자, 가까운 일본에서도 30년 이상 사랑받고 있는 책입니다. 시간이 흘러 세상은 변해도 이 책의 가치는 여전히 빛나고 있습니다.

저자인 I.A 리처드(1983~1979)는 20세기 영어권 문예비평가로 언어 감각의 달인으로 평가받았습니다. 그는 1930년부터 8년 동안 중국에 머물며 영어와 영문학을 가르쳤고, 1940년대에는 미국 메사추세스 주에서 외국인에게 영어를 가르치기도 했습니다.

리처드는 이렇게 오랫동안 영어를 가르치면서 '모국어 간섭 없이 영어를 배우는 것이 좋다'는 생각을 하게 되었다고 합니다. 그 뒤 많은 실험과 연구를 통해 단계적 직접법(Graded Direct Method)이란 학습법을 만들게 되었고, 그 학습법을 기반으로 이 책은 탄생하였습니다.

일본에는 이 학습법이 1947년 동경여자대학 교수 콘스타스 차펠에 의해 소개되었고, 그 뒤 하버드 대학에서 리처드에게 직접 배운 요시자와 미에가 교사 양성 트레이닝을 시작하며 본격적으로 활성화되기도 했습니다. 일본에서는 지금까지도 'GDM 영어 교수법 연구회'에 의해 연구 활동이 이어지고 있을 만큼 훌륭한 학습법으로 자리 잡았습니다.

이렇듯 현장에서 50년 이상 폭넓은 조사와 테스트가 이어지면서 책의 내용이 학습법과 더욱 발전하였고, 이 책을 통해 몇 백만 명에 달하는 전 세계의 독자가 이미 영어를 배우는데 성공하였습니다.

세상에서 가장 쉽고 간단히 영어를 끝낼 수 있는 책으로 평가받는 이 책을 펼치는 순간 깜짝 놀라실 겁니다. 한글 해석은 하나도 없고 오로지 영어 문장과 그림만 있기 때문이죠. 그리고 자신도 모르게 영어와 그림을 보며 책장을 넘기는 자신을 발견하고는 한 번 더 놀라게 될 겁니다.
우리는 단어를 모르더라도 손짓과 발짓으로 많은 걸 표현할 수 있지요. 이 책에는 그런 손짓 발짓 영어가 아주 심플한 그림으로 표현되어 있습니다. 나를 가리키며 I라고 말하고, 상대방을 가리키며 You라고 말하는 것 그대로를 그림으로 표현해놓은 것이죠. 이렇게 그림으로 모든 걸 명쾌하게 표현했기 때문에 해석을 거치지 않아도 영어를 이해할 수 있는 거랍니다. 여러분은 그림과 문장을 반복해서 보기만 하면 됩니다.

영어 스피킹을 어떻게 시작해야 할지 막막하다면 이 책은 아주 특별해보일 겁니다. 적은 단어로도 웬만한 표현을 다 말할 수 있기 때문이죠. 또 그림을 흉내 내고 MP3를 입으로 따라하면서 혼자 스피킹 연습을 할 수 있기에 더욱 매력적이라고 할 수 있습니다. 여러분은 어느 정도의 스피킹 실력을 갖추고 싶으세요? 이 책은 일상생활에 지장이 없을 정도의 내용을 담았습니다. 외국인과 일상 대화를 자연스럽게 하고 싶은 사람들을 위한 이 책은 편안한 영어 스피킹을 할 수 있도록 도울 것입니다.

ABOUT THIS BOOK

적은 단어로 스피킹을 완성한다.

말하기를 위한 최고의 책이다. 어떤 언어든지 말을 잘 하려면 자주 듣고 읽어서 많이 알아야 하듯, 이 책 역시 그 원리가 구현되도록 했습니다. 반복해서 읽고, 말해보고, MP3를 활용해 들으면서 따라해보면 자연스럽게 스피킹 능력이 향상되는 것을 느낄 겁니다. 학습자의 수준과 환경에 따라 다르겠지만 기초 실력이 있는 대부분의 사람들은 한 달 정도면 웬만한 표현은 다 말할 수 있을 것입니다.

중학교 수준의 단어로 구성했다. English Re-start 시리즈(이하ER)는 가능한 적은 단어로 일상생활을 표현할 수 있게 했습니다. ER에는 300개의 단어가 ER Advanced 1권에는 ER에 나온 300단어와 새로운 단어 450개를 포함 750단어가 사용되었습니다. 그리고 이 750개의 단어는 ER Advanced 2권에서 1000개의 단어를 자유롭게 사용하기 위한 기초가 됩니다. 쉽고 중요한 단어부터 순서대로 반복하여 등장하기 때문에 무리하게 외우지 않아도 자연스럽게 기억됩니다. 이 단어들만 알아도 영어 커뮤니케이션은 전혀 문제없습니다.

단순한 그림으로 이해력을 높인다 이 책의 그림은 문장의 의미를 선명하게 보여주기 위해 최대한 단순하게 그렸습니다. 각 문장을 선으로 그린 그림으로 표현하여 학습자가 문장의 패턴이나 단어에 집중할 수 있도록 배려했습니다.

자연스럽게 반복학습이 가능하다 이 책은 한 페이지에서 배운 말이나 문장이 다음 페이지의 단어나 문장을 배우는 데 도움이 되도록 구성하였습니다. 앞에서 배운 내용을 뒤에서 반복하는 동시에 새로운 내용을 추가로 배우기 때문에 따로 복습하지 않아도 됩니다. 읽다 보면 자연스럽게 이해하고 기억하게 될 것입니다.

Question과 Workbook은 보너스 이 책은 본문과 Question, Workbook으로 나뉩니다. 본문은 그림과 영어문장만으로 이루어진 부분을 가리키며 대부분의 페이지를 차지합니다. 하지만 내가 확실히 알고 있는지 점검하기 위해 Question, Workbook 코너를 따로 두었습니다. 이 두 코너는 정답을 쓰면서 확인한 후 소리 내어 말해보면 더욱 효과가 큽니다.

이 책의 간단한 활용법 그림과 문장을 가볍게 끝까지 훑어보는 것이 중요합니다. 그림은 오른쪽 순서대로 보세요. 그 다음 소리 내어 읽어보세요. 외우려 하지 말고 몇 번만 반복해서 읽어보세요. 머릿속에 그림이 떠오르고, 입으로는 말을 하게 될 겁니다. Question과 Workbook 코너를 통해 자신의 실력을 확인해보는 것도 좋습니다. 무료로 제공되는 MP3를 들으면서 따라 말해보세요. 아울러 책에 나와 있는 그림을 크게 모션을 취하면서 따라 말해보면 더욱 좋습니다.

MP3는 cafe.naver.com/newrun 에서 다운로드 받을 수 있습니다.

BETA TESTER I

하루만에 회화학원 3개월 다닌 느낌이 나요!

이 책을 한국에 소개하면서 〈ENGLISH RE-START 체험단〉이란 이름으로
독자 여러분을 초대하여 일주일 정도 공부하는 자리를 마련했습니다.
참여해주신 서현지(여/23살/대학생) 씨가 올려준 내용을 요약 소개합니다.

첫째 날! **회화 학원 3개월 다닌 효과가 느껴지던데요.** 첫날은 지하철에서 책을 훑어보는 것부터 시작했어요. 옆에 사람이 신기한 듯 책을 계속 쳐다보더군요. 아주 간단한 그림과 문장을 연결시켜놓았는데 아무리 공부해도 감이 안 잡히던 other, another 등 이런 말들이 뭐랄까 감이 잡히더라고요. 왜 회화학원 다녀도 머리로는 아는데 입으로는 안 나오던 문장들 있잖아요. 그런 말들을 나도 모르게 중얼거리게 되더라고요. 무엇보다 회화에 자신감이 생겨 좋았습니다. 덧붙이면 저희 어머니께서 이 책을 보시더니 출판되면 꼭 하나 사달라고 하시더라고요. 재미있고 쉬워 보였나봅니다! 나중엔 엄마랑 같이 공부해야겠어요~

둘째, 셋째 날! **헷갈리는 단어가 그림으로 다 생각나요.** 영어 문장은 복잡해졌는데도 그림은 계속 간결하네요! 오늘은 어제 배운 것들도 나와서 자연스럽게 복습하였고 새로운 단어, 문법, 문장도 배울 수 있었습니다. take off란 동사는 매번 생각이 잘 안 났는데 오늘 그림 한 컷으로 확실히 정리가 되었어요. 이렇게 헷갈리는 단어, 숙어들이 그림으로 기억되면서 책을 덮어도 다 생각나는 거예요. 전치사도 헷갈리지 않게 복습할 수 있어서 좋았습니다! 근데 이 그림, 볼수록 맘에 들어요~

넷째 날! **영어회화에 많이 쓰이는 단어가 보여요.** 오늘 공부한 부분은 회화에 도움이 많이 될 것 같네요. 앞에 나온 내용이 반복되면서 새로운 내용이 등장해 저절로 복습이 되더라구요. 특히 짧은 문장에서 서서히 긴 문장으로 확장되면서 단어들이 반복되니까 그 단어의 의미도 정확히 알게 되었고, 단어들의 시제 변화까지 볼 수 있었답니다. 이야기가 짧은 꽁트 같아서 책 보는 재미도 쏠쏠 했어요!

다섯째, 여섯째 날! **발음이 고쳐져요.** 오늘은 MP3파일을 들으면서 했는데요. 처음에는 MP3속도가 좀 느리단 생각이 들었어요. 그런데 들으면서 따라해보니 속도가 딱 적당하더라구요. 발음도 정확해서 발음 교정에도 좋을 것 같습니다. 집에서 들을 때는 실제로 그림처럼 행동을 해봤는데 처음에는 민망하다가 나중에는 재밌어졌어요. 그러고 나니 확실하게 기억되어 죽어도 안 까먹을 것 같더라구요.^^ 외우려고 하지 않아도 자연스럽게 외워지는 것 같아서 기분이 좋았답니다.

마지막 날! **문법, 단어, 듣기, 말하기 한 번에 되요** 책으로 공부하고, 지하철이나 버스 안에서 MP3를 듣고 중얼거리면서 복습하기에 딱 좋은 것 같아요. 내용이 어렵지 않아서 그런지 책 없이 MP3만 듣고도 그림이 떠오르는 장면이 꽤 있었어요! 나도 모르게 떠오르는 그림들을 생각하면서 정말 신기했답니다! 아무래도 이 책의 가장 큰 장점은 문법, 단어, 듣기, 말하기를 한 번에 연습할 수 있다는 거 같아요. 주변 사람들에게 완전 추천해주고 싶습니다. 특히 저희 부모님? 특별한 영어공부 해보게 돼서 너무 좋았어요!

BETA TESTER II

영어 한 달만 다시 해봐야겠어요!

〈ENGLISH RE-START 체험단〉 활동에 참여해주신 분들이 남겨주신 글입니다.

온몸으로 하는 영어 공부, 적극 추천! 직접 모자와 테이블을 갖다 놓고 문장을 읽어보며 해봤는데, 훨씬 더 그림을 이해하기 쉬웠습니다. 와~ 정말 신기해요!

– 이춘호, 남, 31세, 회사원, kjj2949

put on, 더 이상 헷갈리지 않아요! 쉽지만 항상 헷갈렸던 put on 같은 숙어들이 워크북을 공부하면서 깔끔하게 정리 되었습니다. 여기에 나와 있는 표현들을 잘 익혀두면 토익에 큰 도움이 될 듯싶네요!

– 최광식, 남, 28세, 고시생, lumplant

시제 고민은 이제 그만! 제가 생각한 베스트 컷은 English Re-start 38~39 page의 그림이었어요. 한글 설명 없이도 이해가 되다니…. 다양한 행동과 연속적인 그림을 통해서 시제 변화와 개념을 확실히 알게 되었어요.

– 김경자, 여, 38세, 회사원, flqj1004

자연산 영어 그대로를 즐기는 방법! 그림으로 보는 게 해석된 문장을 보는 것보다 은근히 해석이 쉬워요. 그동안 영어를 배웠던 느낌과는 전혀 달라요. 진짜 영어가 흡수되는 느낌? 아주 좋아요!

– 김재희, 여, 33세, 컨설턴트, jesusbarag17

10년 묵은 '관사' 체증, 이제야 풀리네요! 영어 공부를 하다가 제일 헷갈리는 게 a, the 등 관사인데, 이 책만큼 쉽게 관사의 느낌을 이해하게 되는 책은 처음 봤어요. 그림과 문장만 봤을 뿐인데, 아아 관사가 이런 거구나 싶더라고요.

– 오재학, 남, 24세, 대학생, happyjjory

소리 내서 공부하니 발음도 잡히네요! 소리를 내면서 읽었는데, 상당한 효과가 있더군요. 쉬운 문장이긴 하지만 억양이라든가 발음에 있어서도 다시 한번 잡아준다는 느낌도 받았고요. 진작 이렇게 공부했으면 지금쯤 발음 걱정 없을 텐데 말이죠!

– 진우경, 남, 29세, 마케터, goorm1226

자투리 시간에 딱이에요! 지하철에서 작게 소리 내어 읽으면서 공부했는데, 자투리 시간을 활용해서 영어 공부도 하니 도착지까지 시간이 금세 가더군요! 새롭게 알게 된 표현들도 많았습니다.

– 유모란, 여, 25세, 취업준비생 rhaxodn

눈 딱 감고 한 달만 다시 해보려고요! 영어 공부를 한 지가 정말 오래되서 어디서부터 다시 시작해야 할지 막막했는데... 이 책을 보면서 영어를 이렇게 다시 시작할 수도 있겠다는 용기를 얻었네요! 눈 딱 감고 한 달만 해볼랍니다! 아자!

– 정영희, 여, 51세, 주부, jyh0212

CONTENTS

English Re-start Advanced 1 for speaking

English Re-start

Advanced 1 for speaking

This is a bedroom.
There are two beds in it.

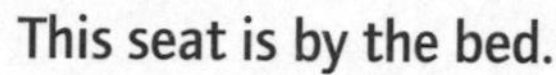

This seat is by the bed.

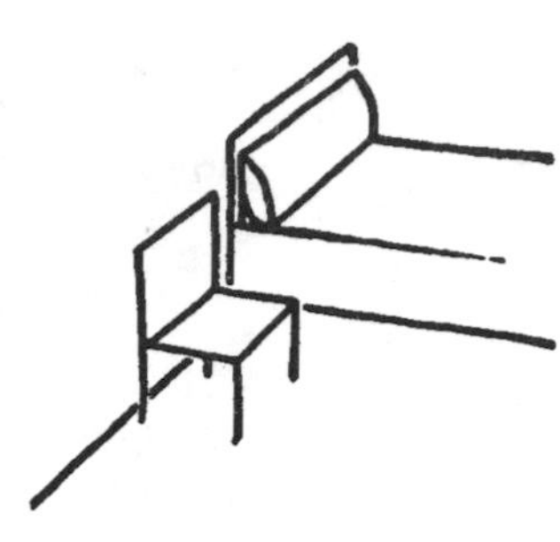

What is on the seat?
A bag is on the seat.

A woman is by the bed.
Who is she?
She is Mrs. Smith.

What is she doing?

She is putting things into the bag.

What is she putting into the bag?

She is putting Mr. Smith's things into it.

Mr. Smith is going to California. Mr. and Mrs. Smith are in New York State.

He will go by train. This is a train. From New York State to California is a long journey.

What will he take with him to California?

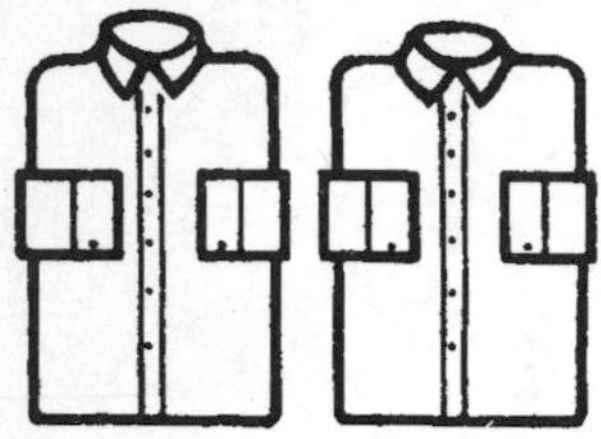

He will take some shirts.

He will take some socks.

He will not take old socks. Old socks have holes in them.

He will take new socks. New socks have no holes in them.

These trousers have a hole in them. They are old trousers.

He will take some shoes.

He will put them in a shoe bag.

The shoe bag will keep the other things clean.

The bag is between the shoes and the shirt. The shoes will not make the shirt dirty.

My hands are dirty..

My hands are clean.

This cloth is dirty.

This cloth is clean.

This plate is clean.

This plate is dirty.

His face is dirty.

His face is clean.

The plate is dirty but the cloth is clean.

Now the cloth is dirty but the plate is clean.

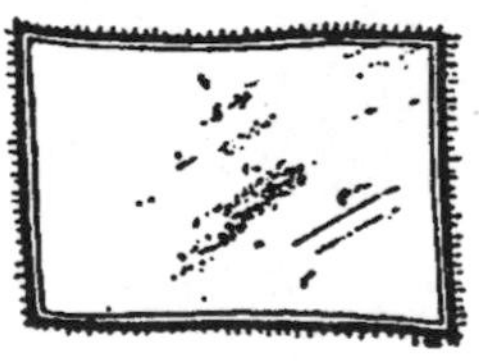

This is a basin.

This is warm water in it.

This is soap.

What is she doing?

She is washing her hands with soap and warm water.

Her hands are wet now but they are clean. They were dirty.

What is she doing?

She is drying her hands on a cloth.

Her hands were wet.

Now they are dry. They were dirty. Now they are clean.

What is this?

It is a brush. It is a toothbrush.

What is this?

It is toothpaste.

She is putting some toothpaste on the brush.

Now she is brushing her teeth.

Her teeth will be clean. They will be clean and white.

What is this?
It is a comb.

And this?

It is a brush.
It is a hairbrush.

She is brushing her hair.

Now she is combing her hair.

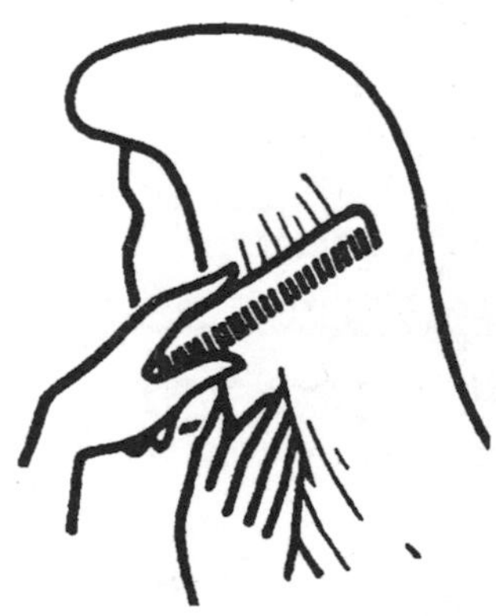

What are these?

They are pins.

One pin is very like another pin.

This pin.

is like this pin.

But they are two pins. They are not the same pin. They are different pins.

These are three hairpins. They are different hairpins.

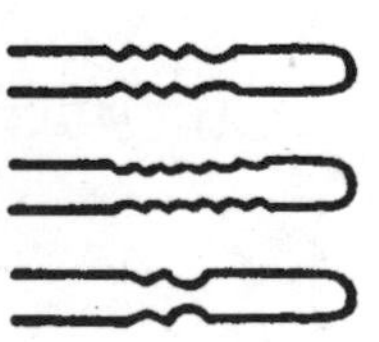

She has a hairpin in her hand.
She is putting it in her hair.

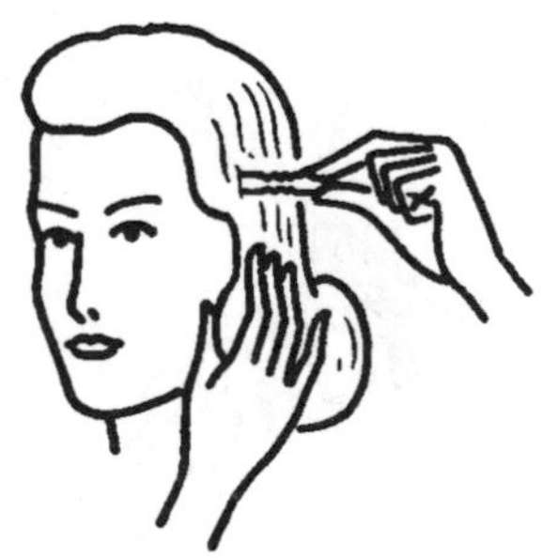

Now it is in her hair.
It was in her hand.
It is in her hair now.
But it is the same hairpin.

He is brushing his hair.
He does not put pins in his hair.

Mrs. Smith put some shirts and some socks and shoes (in a shoe bag) and a comb and brushes and toothpaste and soap and a wash cloth in Mr. Smith's bag.

She put all these things in his bag.

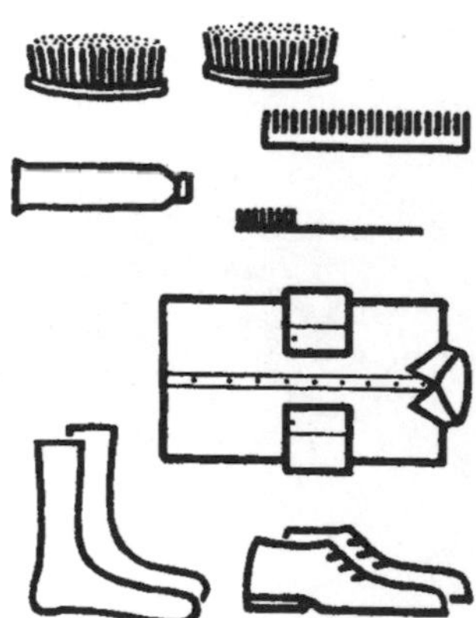

Mr. Smith will go to the station in a taxi.

This is a taxi.
Mr. Smith is getting into it.
He has his bag with him.

This is the station.

The taxi is in front of the station.
The time is 8:00.
The train will go at 8:30.

Mr. Smith is getting out of the taxi.

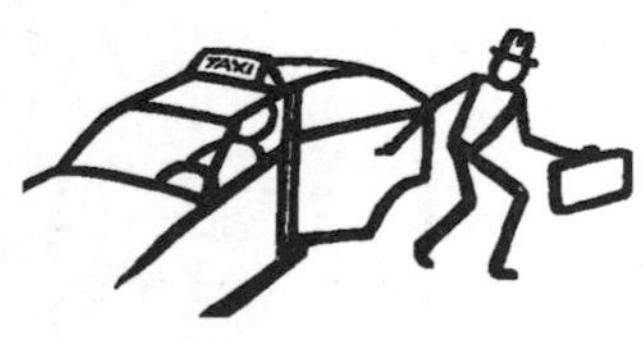

Now he is going into the station.

This is the waiting room in the station.

Those men and women on the seats in the waiting room are waiting. They are waiting for their trains.

Here is a train.

This is the engine of a train.

This is the bell on the engine.

These are rails. The train goes on these rails. It is a railroad train.

Here is the ticket office in the station.

Mr. Smith got his ticket here.

Here is his ticket. He gave $841.80 for his ticket.

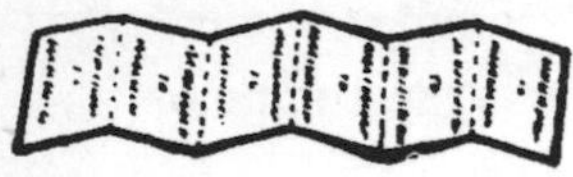

These are tickets.

How much was his ticket for the journey to Los Angeles?
It was eight hundred and forty-one dollars and eighty cents ($841.80).

How long is the journey?
Four days.
Which days will he be on the train?
He will be on the train Sunday, Monday, Tuesday, Wednesday.
The other days of the week are Thursday, Friday, Saturday.

How much money did he take with him for his journey?
He took five hundred and nineteen dollars ($519.00).
Much money: $5000
Little money: $5

Mr. Smith has friends in California.

Mr. Smith His friends

Here are his friends.
He and his friends are shaking hands.
(See page 134.)

His friends were waiting for him at the station.

They say, "Did you have a good journey?"
He says, "Yes, but it was a long journey."

His friend says, "Let me have your bag, please."
He will go with his friends to their house.

This is a letter: a.
These are letters: a, b, c.
This is a word: man.
Three letters make the word *man*.
The man is writing a letter. He is writing on paper with a pen.

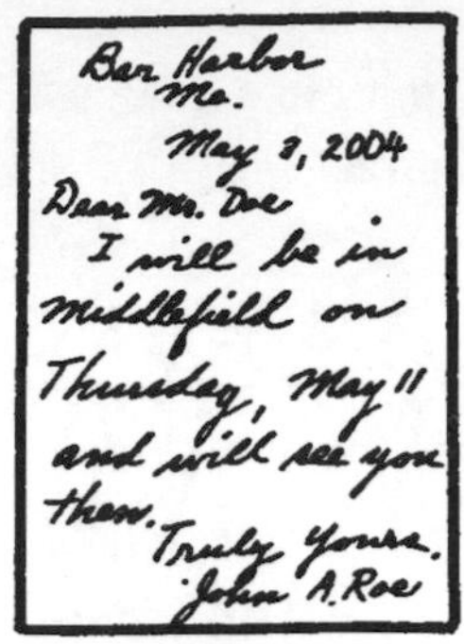

Bar Harbor
Me.
May 3, 2004
Dear Mr. Doe
I will be in Middlefield on Thursday, May 11 and will see you then.
Truly yours,
John A. Roe

This is the letter.
It is in Mr. Roe's writing.
Mr. Roe will send the letter to Mr. Doe.

Here is the letter ready for the post.

Here is the stamp.

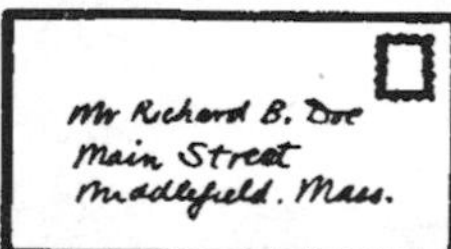

Mr. Doe's name and street and town are on the letter.
Mass. is short for Massachusetts.
Middlefield is in Massachusetts.

This is the back of the letter.
Mr. Roe's name, and the town where he is living

are on the back of the letter.
Me. is short for Maine.
Bar Harbor is in Maine.
Massachusetts and Maine are two states of the United States of America.

Mr. Smith is writing a card to Mrs. Smith. He is in San Francisco. On one side of the card is a picture of the harbor. Here is the picture. This is a picture postcard.

Here is the other side of the card. Mr. Smith is putting Mrs. Smith's name on it.

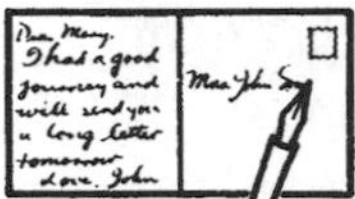

He will put her street under the name. He will put her town under the street. Then he will put the state where her town is.

Now the card is ready for the post.

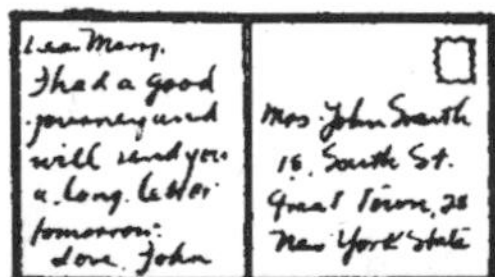

There is a stamp on the card. Mrs. Smith's name and street and town are on the right hand side of the card. Mrs. Smith's town is in New York State.

Mr. Smith is taking the card to the post office. He is going up the steps.

He will put the card in the letter box on the wall of the post office.

He is sending the card to Mrs. Smith.
This morning Mrs. Smith got the card which Mr. Smith sent to her from San Francisco.
She is reading it now.
She is reading: "I had a good journey...."

Reading and writing are parts of our education.
We get a great part of our education at school.
These boys and girls are at school.
The teacher is teaching them.

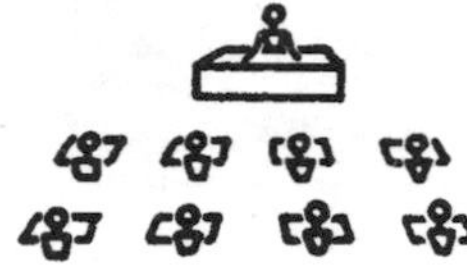

Mrs. Smith is sending Jane and Tom to school.

They will be at school before nine.
They get good teaching at school.

At school, Tom and Jane are learning.
They were reading and now they are writing.

Tom is writing the word *learning* on the board.
The teacher is teaching him the word *learning*.

Now Tom and Jane are back from school. Jane is reading a story.

It is eight-thirty.

Tom is writing at the table.

Tom's dog is at his feet.

Mrs. Smith is reading the newspaper.

Tom and Jane are getting a good education.

They get some of it at school, and they get some of it from their mother and father.

Mrs. Smith is taking a look at Tom's work.

It is good work.

Now Mrs. Smith is writing a letter to Mr. Smith. She sends love from Tom and Jane to their father.

Dear John,

We are all well. Tom and Mary are at school. They are doing good work.

She will send the letter to Mr. Smith.

She has the letter in her hand.

Now she is sending the letter.

She sent the letter.

a What are these?

What is this boy doing?

b What are these?

What is the man doing?

c What are these?

What is the girl doing?

d What is this?

What is the woman doing?

The answers are on page **28**.

QUESTIONS

a On page 13, where did Mr. Smith get his ticket?	b How much was the ticket?
c How long was the journey to Los Angeles?	d Did he go in an airplane?
e What did his friends say to him when they saw him?	f What did he say on the card which he sent to Mrs. Smith?
g What are Tom and Jane learning at school?	h What did Mrs. Smith send to Mr. Smith from Tom and Jane?

The answers are on page **28**.

This is a plate.
The plate is round.

This is an orange.
The orange is round.

The face of the clock is round.
The hands of the clock go round.

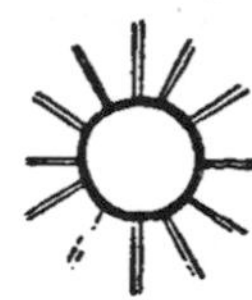

This is the earth.

The earth is round.

This is the moon.

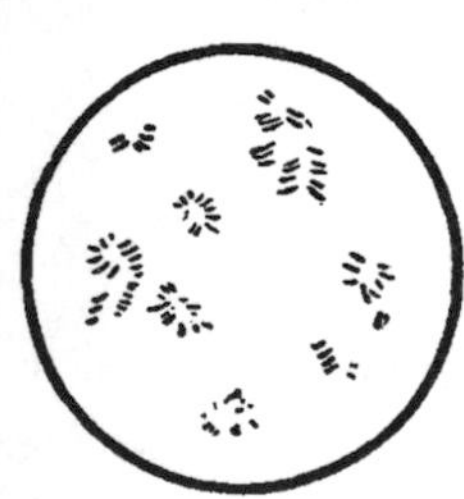

The moon is round.

This is the sun.

This is the sky.

This is a cloud in the sky.

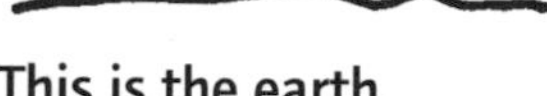

This is the earth.

The sun comes up in the East.

It comes up every morning.

The sun goes down in the West.

It goes down every night.

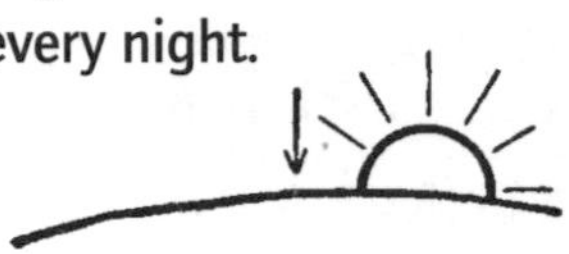

What is the time? It is five-eight A.M.

The sun is coming up now at five-eight (5:08) A.M.

What is the time? It is five-twenty (5:20) P.M.

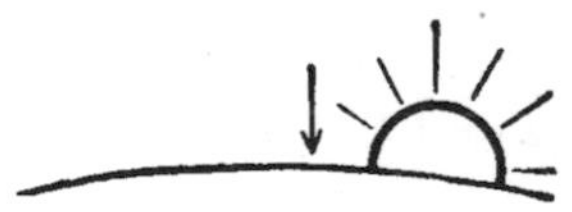

The sun is going down now at five-twenty (5:20) P.M.

Yesterday the sun came up at five-seven (5:07) A.M. and went down at eight-nineteen (8:19) P.M. Today the sun came up at five-six (5:06) A.M. and will go down at eight-twenty (8:20) P.M. Tomorrow it will come up at five-five (5:05) A.M. and will go down at eight twenty-one (8:21).

This is night.

This is the earth.
That is a star.

This is morning.

The sun is coming up.

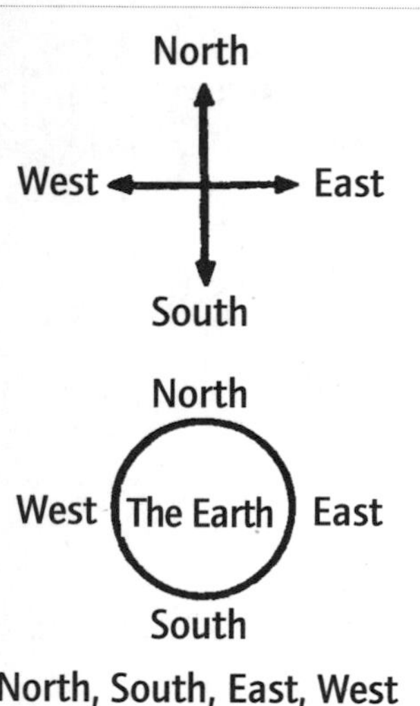

North, South, East, West are four directions.

There are twenty-four hours in one day.
Twenty-four hours make one day.
Two and two make four.
Three and five make eight. What do five and six make?
Do they make ten, or eleven, or twelve?
That is a question.
The answer is "Eleven."

Say these numbers: 1, 2, 3, 4, 5, 6, 7, 8, 9, 10, 11, 12.
What number comes after 12? Thirteen.
What comes after 13? Fourteen.
What comes after 14? Fifteen.

What numbers come after 15?
Sixteen 16
Seventeen 17
Eighteen 18
Nineteen 19
Twenty 20

Twenty 20	Twenty-one 21
Thirty 30	Thirty-one 31
Forty 40	Forty-one 41
Fifty 50	Fifty-one 51
Sixty 60	Seventy 70

Eighty 80 Ninety 90
A hundred 100
A hundred and one 101
A thousand 1000
A million 1,000,000

QUESTIONS What are these things?

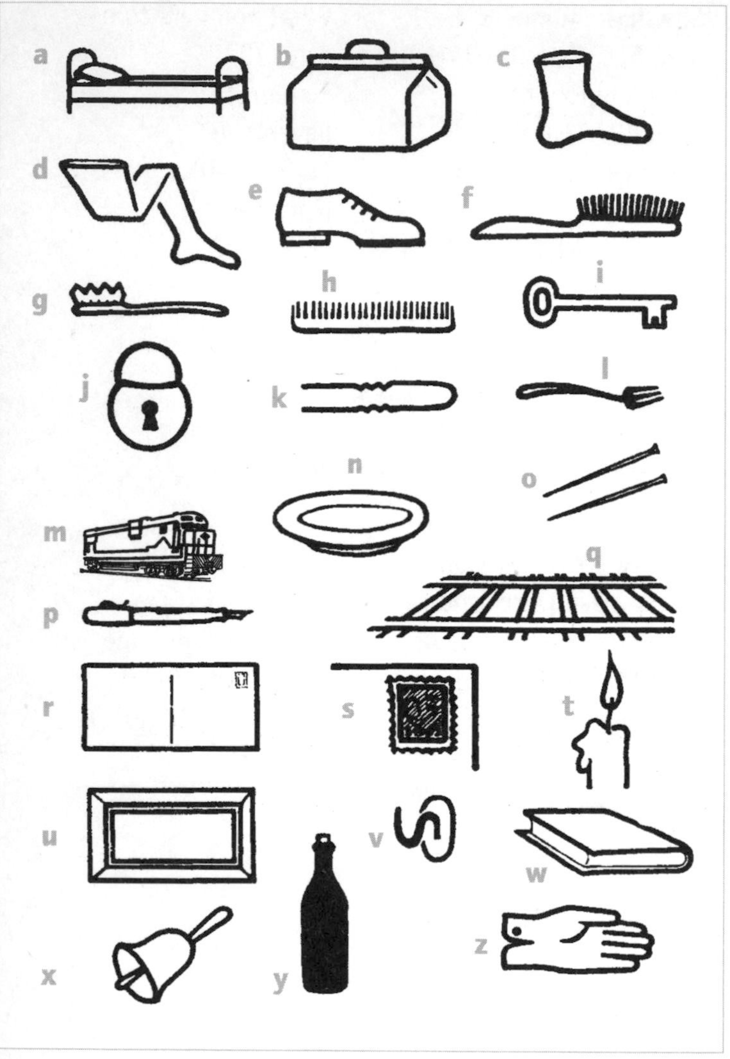

The answers are on page **29**.

QUESTIONS

a What do seven and eleven make?
What do twenty and forty make?
What do thirteen and thirty make?
What do two hundred and three and three hundred and four make?

b Where does the sun come up and where does it go down?
Does day come after night?
Does night come after day?

c This is a letter.
Where do we put Mr. Green's street and town and state on the letter?

d Tom's work at school is learning.
He is a learner.
What is the teacher's work?

The answers are on page **29**.

Page 20

a They are shoes.
He is putting his shoes on his feet.

b They are shirts.
He is putting his things in his bag.

c They are toothpaste and a toothbrush.
She is brushing her teeth.

d It is soap.
She is washing her hands.

Page 21

a He got his ticket at the ticket office in the station.

b The ticket was $841.80.

c The journey was four days long.

d No. He did not go in an airplane. He went in a train.

e They said, "Did you have a good journey?"

f He said, "I had a good journey and will send you a long letter tomorrow. Love. John."

g They are learning reading and writing at school.

h She sent love from Tom and Jane.

Page 26

a a bed	b a bag	c a sock
d a stocking	e a shoe	f a hairbrush
g a toothbrush	h a comb	i a key
j a lock	k a hairpin	l a fork
m an engine	n a plate	o two pins
p a pen	q rails	r a card
s a stamp	t a flame	u a frame
v a hook	w a book	x a bell
y a bottle	z a glove	

Page 27

a Eighteen. Sixty. Forty-three. Five hundred and seven.

b The sun comes up in the East and goes down in the West.
Yes, day comes after night.
Yes, night comes after day.

c We put his street under his name and we put the name of the town under the name of the street. And under that we put the name of the state.

d The teacher's work is teaching.

This boy's name is Tom.

This girl's name is Jane.

Tom is making something.

Jane is saying, "What are you making, Tom?"

Tom is saying, "I am making a house."

This is a box.

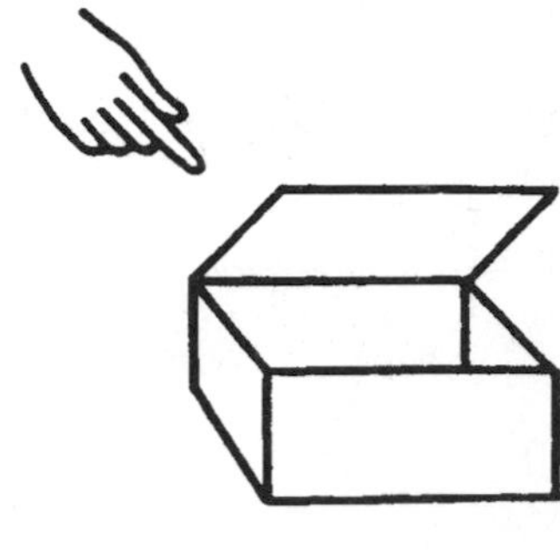

This is one side of the box.

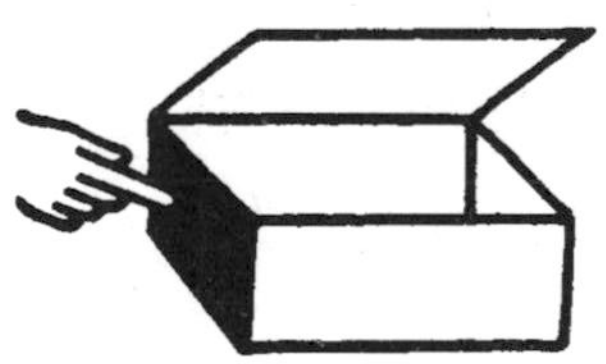

This is the opposite side of the box.

This is the front of the box.

And this is the back of the box.

This is the floor of the box.

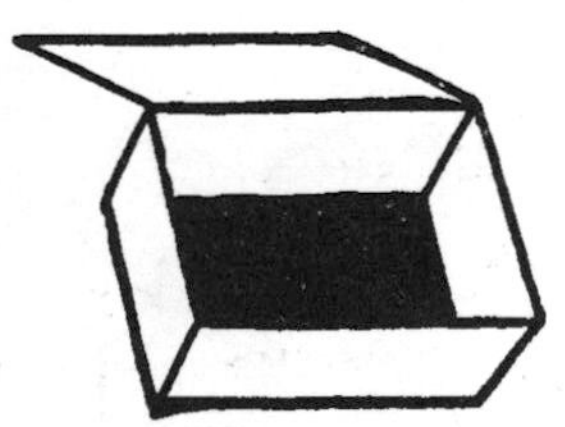

And this is the cover of the box.

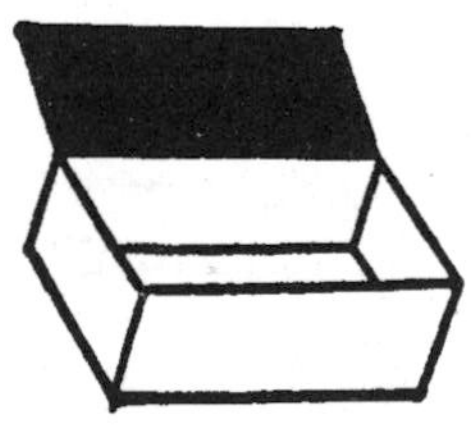

Now this side will be one wall of the house.

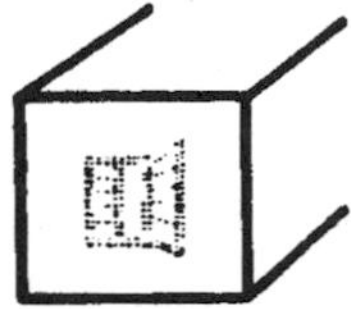

I will put a window in here.

This will be the opposite wall of the house.

I will put another window in this opposite wall.

The front of the box will be the front of the house.

I will put a step under the door.

This is a step.

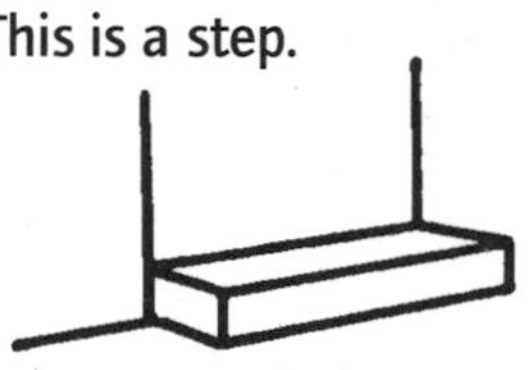

These are steps.

Three steps.

Jane said, "A house has a roof. Will you put a roof on the house? How will you make the roof?"

I will make the roof from the cover of the box.

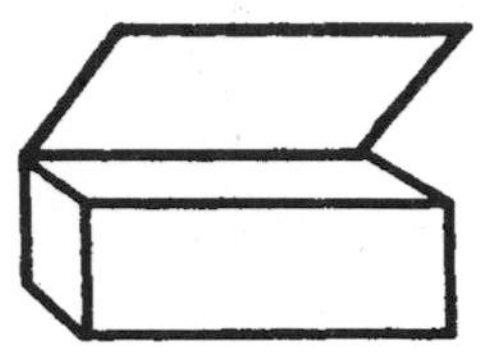

No. There is not enough wood in the cover.

How long is the cover?

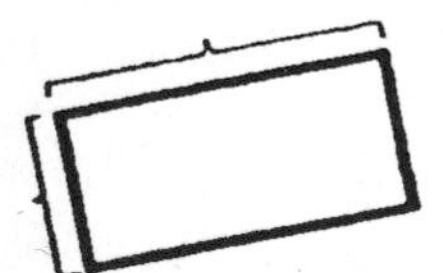

How wide is the cover?

I am measuring it.

The cover is not long enough.
It is not wide enough.

The roof is like this.

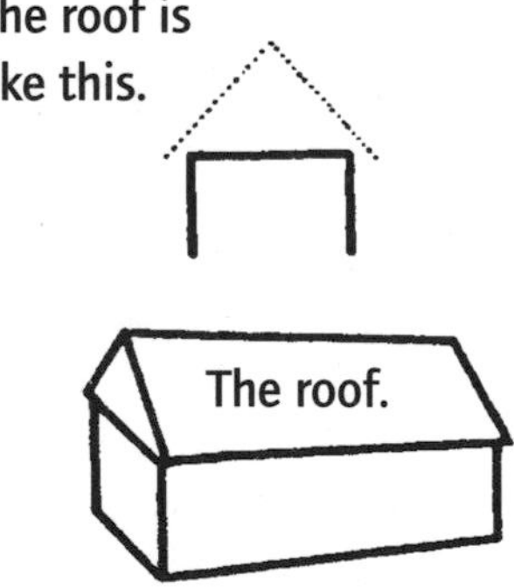

Here is a wider bit of wood.

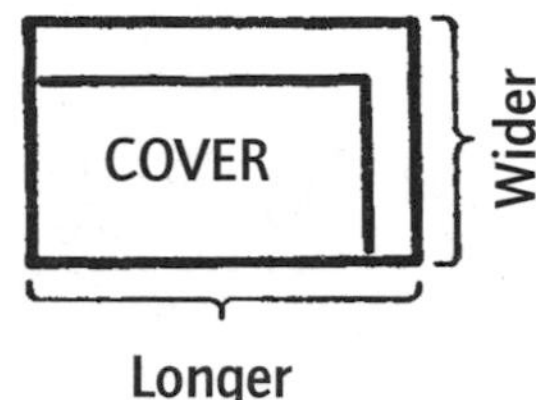

It is wider and it is longer.

I will make the roof from this other bit of wood.

I will make a cut in this wood.

I will make a cut at this angle.

A cut.

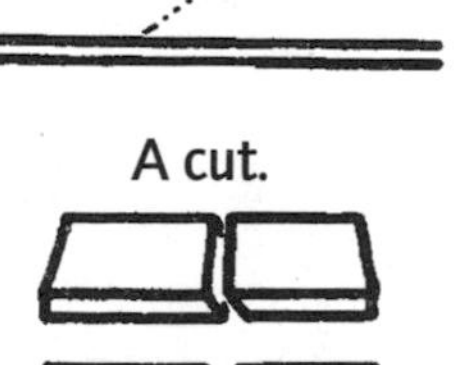

This is an angle.

This is an angle.

This is a right angle.

This is another right angle.

"What are you doing, Tom?"
"I am measuring the wood."

It is good wood.

This is a measure.

We get wood from trees.

These are trees.

Some wood is hard. Some wood is soft.

This is a tree.

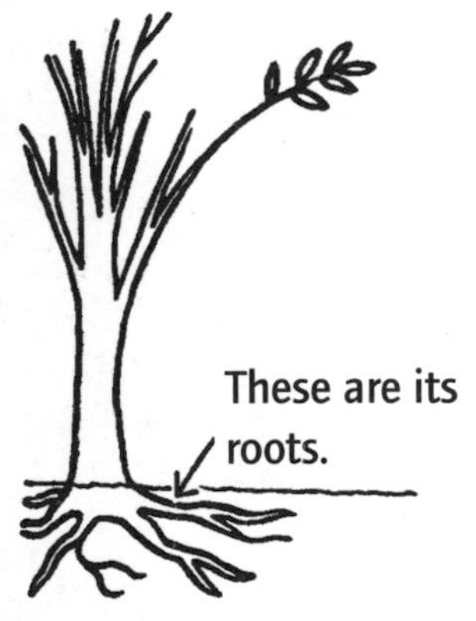

We get hard wood from some trees.

They give hard wood to us.

Other trees give soft wood to us.

Now I am making a cut at this angle in this bit of wood.

The blade is going through the wood.

This is my knife.

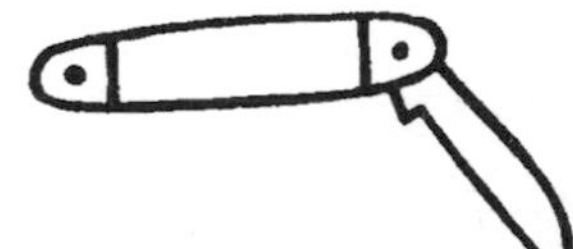

This is the blade of my knife.

I am making a line on the wood.
I am making a line with a pencil.

This is the pencil.

This is the line.

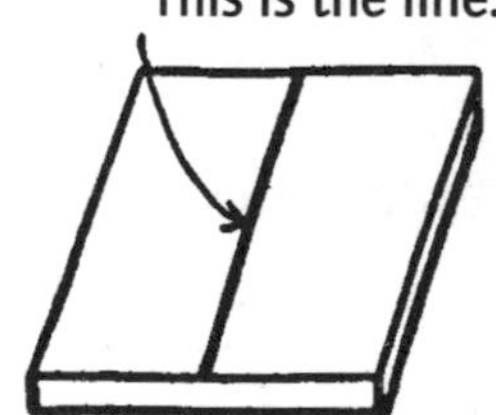

"Keep on the line when you are cutting. Don't go off it."

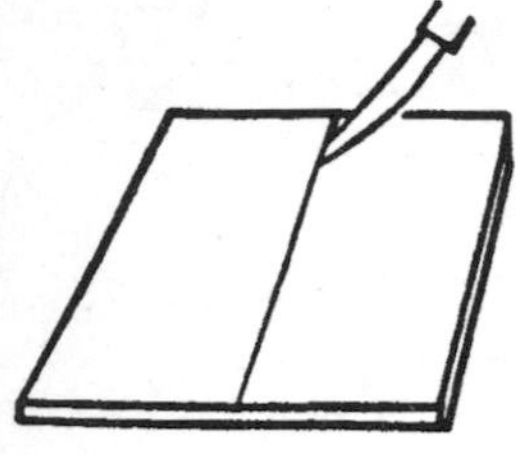

That is bad! The cut is off the line.

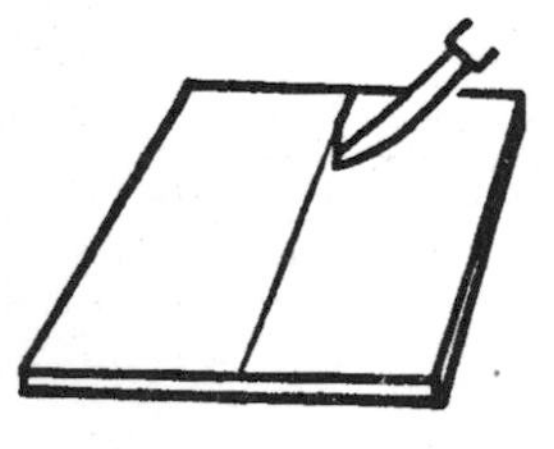

It's not very bad.

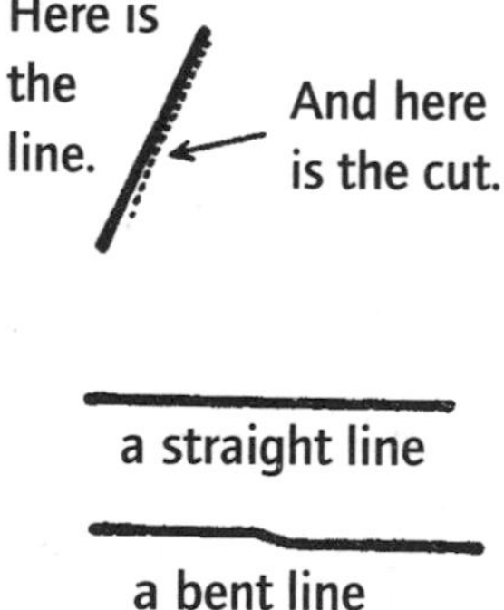

Tom is making another attempt.

That is better. The cut is straight. The blade of the knife went straight. Good!

Now I have these two bits of wood.

I will put them together like this.

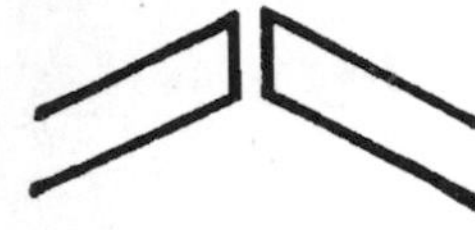

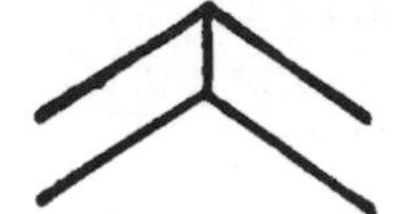

There is the roof of the house.

Now I will put the two parts of the roof together with nails.

These are nails.

I will make a hole through this part of the roof into the other part of the roof.

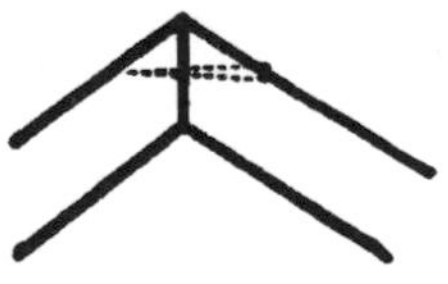

Tom is making the holes for the nails.

Now he is putting the nails in with his hammer.

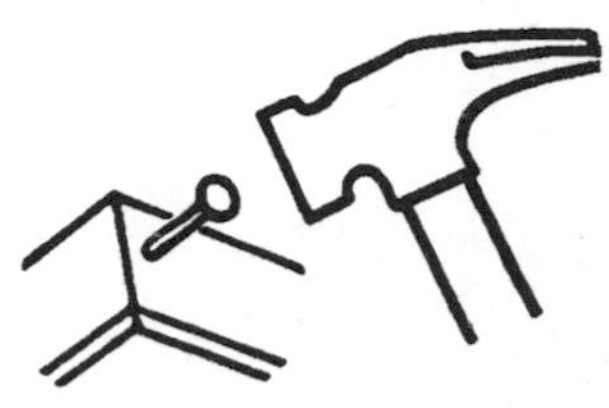

Now the two parts of the roof are together.

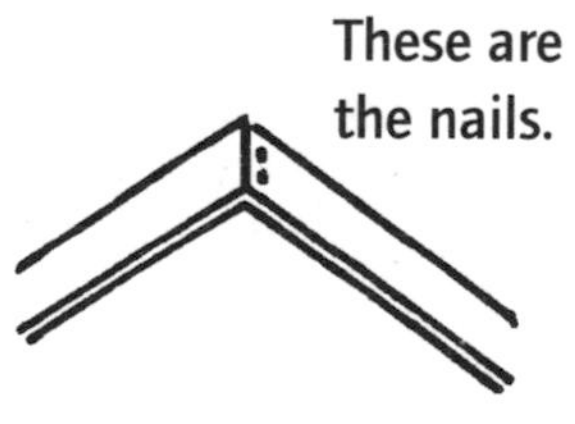

The roof is ready.

Is this line long?

This line is longer.

Is this bit of wood strong?

This bit of wood is stronger.

Here are the supports for the roof.

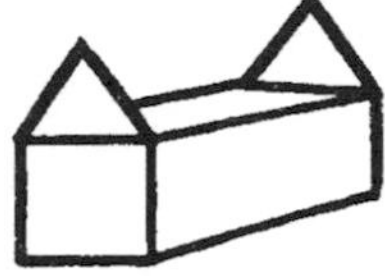

Will you put another support for it in the middle?

Where?

Here.

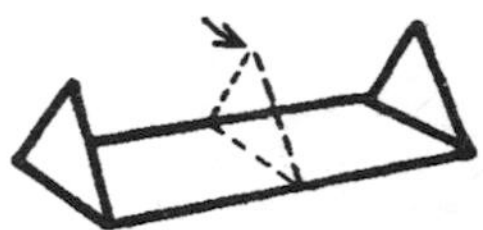

In the middle.

Yes, that is better.

This is a straight line.

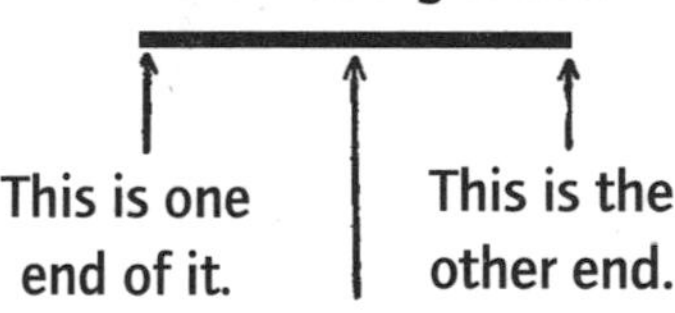

This is one end of it.

This is the other end.

This is the middle of it.

This is a bent line.

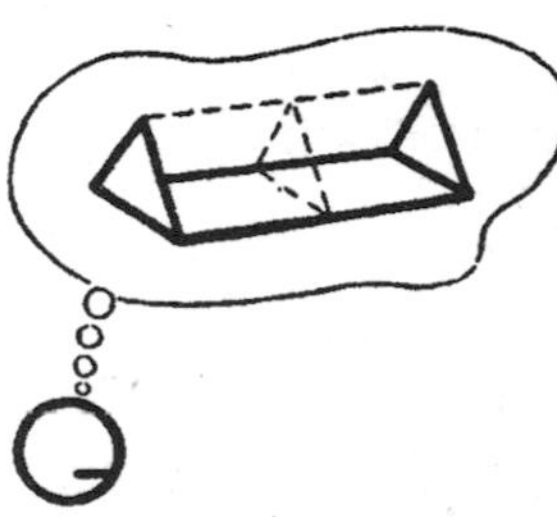

That will be better. That will make the roof stronger.

Jane is making something.

I am making a coat and trousers.

Here are the trousers.

Here is the coat.

"Has your coat a collar?"

"Yes, it has. Here is the collar."

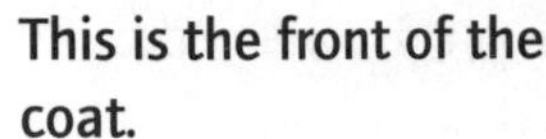

This is the front of the coat.

Here is the collar of the coat.

This is the back of the coat.

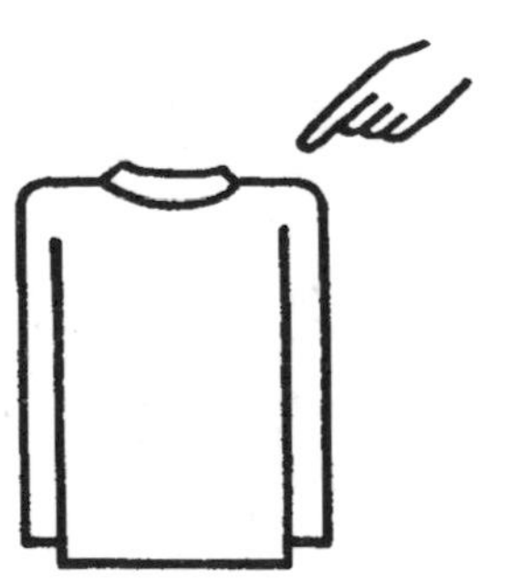

This is one side of it.

This is one pocket of it.

Here is the other side.

These are the arms of the coat.

These are the buttons of the coat.

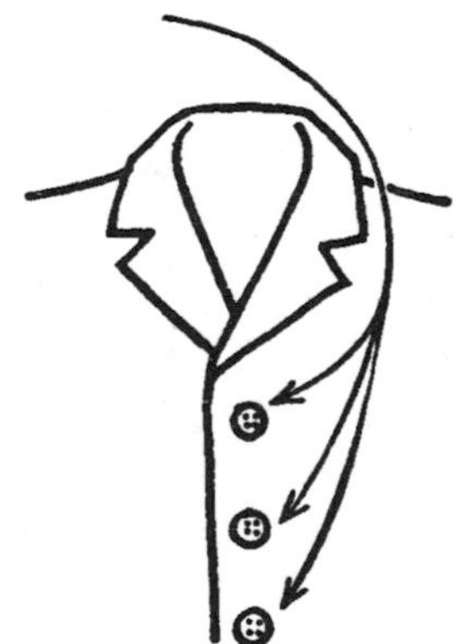

This is a button.

This is a button-hole.

This is a needle.

This is thread.

What are you doing with your needle now?

I am putting this button on the coat.

And I am making the button-holes.

The girl will put the end of the thread through the needle.

She has the needle in the fingers of one hand and the thread in the fingers of the other hand.

This is the end of the thread.

This is the hole in the needle.

It is the eye of the needle.

The end of the thread is not going straight. It is not going through the hole in the needle.

The thread did not go through the needle. It is not through the hole in the needle now.

It is on one side of the needle.

It is on this side of the needle.

Now the girl is doing it again.
Is the end of the thread through the hole?
No, it is not.
It is on the other side of the needle.

The girl is making another attempt.
This time the thread will go through the hole.
The end of the thread is straight.

It went through.
The girl is taking the end of the thread in her fingers.
The thread is through the needle.

Where are your scissors?
Here they are.

This blade is narrow. This blade is wide.

Narrow?
This is a narrow street.

This is a wide street.

These trousers are wide.

These trousers are narrow.

QUESTIONS

a These are two walls.

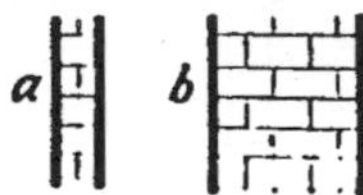

Which of them is thicker?
Is wall *a* or wall *b* thicker?

b These are two cuts.

Which of them is wider?
Is cut *a* or cut *b* wider?

c These are two nails.

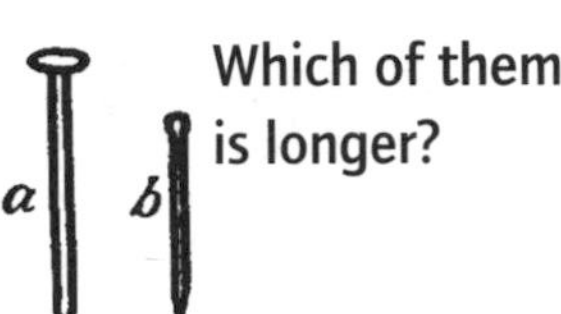

Which of them is longer?

d Which of these two men is stronger?

e Which of these two pencils is shorter?

f Which of these two cards is longer?

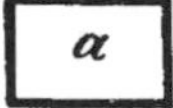

Which is wider?

g Which of these three angles is a right angle?

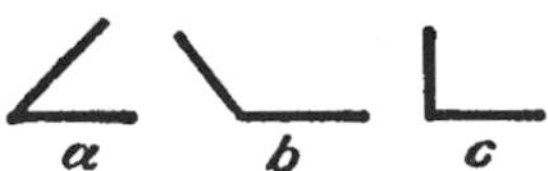

h Which of these things are broken?

The answers are on page **54**.

QUESTIONS

a What is he doing?

b What is she doing?

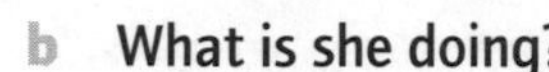

c What is he doing?

d What is he doing now?

e What is he doing?

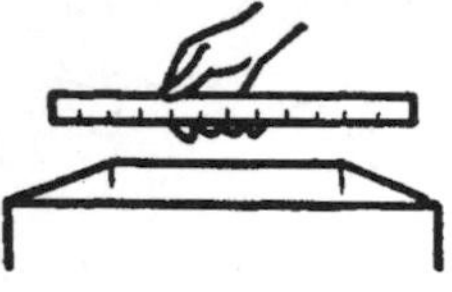

f What is she doing?

g What is she doing now?

h And what is she doing now?

The answers are on page **54**.

A What are these things?

B Which of them go through the air?

C Which of them go on their feet?

D Which of them go on the water?

The answers are on page **54**.

Page 51

a Wall *b* is thicker.
b Cut *b* is wider.
c Nail *a* is longer.
d The man who is on his feet is stronger.
e Pencil *b* is shorter.
f Card *b* is longer.
Card *a* is wider.
g Angle *c* is a right angle.
h The cup, the hammer, and the plate are broken.

Page 52

a He is going up the steps.
b She is going down the steps.
c He is putting a nail in with a hammer.
d He is taking a nail out with a hammer.
e He is measuring a box.
f She is putting a thread through the hole in a needle.
g She is taking the end of the thread between her finger and thumb.
h She is putting a button on with a needle and thread.

Page 53

A

a a train
b its engine
c an airplane
d a seat
e a ship
f a flower
g mountains
h trees
i a star
j a cloud
k the sun
l the moon
m a pig
n a sheep
o a horse
p a cow
q a dog
r a goat
s a coat
t a bird
u trousers
v a cup
w a knife
x a spoon
y scissors

B Airplanes and birds go through the air.
C Pigs, sheep, horses, cows, dogs, birds, and goats go on their feet.
D Ships and some birds go on the water.

The earth goes round in twenty-four hours.

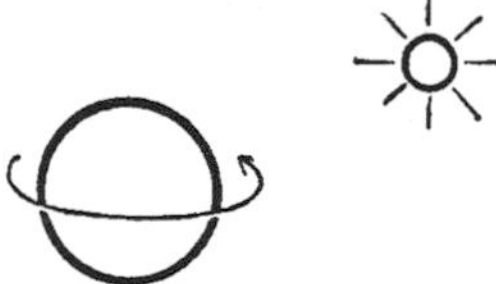

There are twenty-four hours in every day. The sun comes up and goes down every day because the earth is turning round.

The earth goes round the sun in a year.

There are three hundred and sixty-five days in a year. Three hundred and sixty-five days make a year.

There are seven days in a week. Seven days make a week. Here are the names of the days of the week: Monday, Tuesday, Wednesday, Thursday, Friday, Saturday, Sunday. Monday is before Tuesday. Tuesday is after Monday.

There are thirty-one or thirty or twenty-eight days in a month.
Here are the names of the months:
January (31)
February (28)
March (31)
April (30)
May (31)
June (30)
July (31)
August (31)
September (30)
October (31)
November (30)
December (31).
January is before February ...
February is after January...

These are the winter months: December, January, February.
These are the summer months: June, July, August.
These are the spring months: March, April, May.
These are the fall months: September, October, November.

In the North, the earth is cold in the winter.
The wind is cold.
Snow comes down from the sky.
There are no leaves on the trees.
There is ice over the water.
The days are short.

In the North, the earth and the air are warm in the summer. There are leaves on the trees.
The days are long.
There is no ice or snow.

In the spring the leaves come out on the trees.
Plants come up out of the earth, and flowers come out on the plants.

In the fall, the leaves come down from the branches of the trees.
Fall is the time of the fall of the leaves.
They are coming down. They are falling.

In the spring the days get longer.
Every day is longer than the day before it.
In the spring today is longer than yesterday.

In the fall the days get shorter.
Every day is shorter than the day before it.
In the fall tomorrow will be shorter than today.

This line.

is longer than

this line.

The time between three and four is shorter than the time between three and five.

One hour is a shorter time than two hours.

Fifteen minutes make a quarter of an hour.

Thirty minutes make half an hour.

Forty-five minutes make three-quarters of an hour.

Which is shorter-a quarter of an hour or half an hour?

Which is shorter-the minute hand or the hour hand of a clock?

This is an inch.

The distance from A to B is one inch.

Half an inch is a shorter distance than an inch.

A quarter of an inch

Three-quarters of an inch

Twelve inches make a foot.

This is a foot.

How long is it?
It is ten inches long.

Three feet make a yard.

This is a yard measure.

There are thirty-six inches in a yard.

These are feet.

They are not twelve inches long.

Seventeen hundred and sixty yards (1760) make a mile.
In half a mile there are eight hundred and eighty yards.
Miles, yards, feet, and inches are measures of distance.

What are this man and this girl doing?
They are taking a walk.

In one hour he will go two miles, and she will go four miles.
He is slow. She is quick.
She is quicker than he is.
He is slower than she is.

This is a train.

Trains are quicker than horses or men.

This is an airplane.

Airplanes are quicker than trains or horses or men.

This baby is one year old.

This boy is ten years old.

This man is thirty years old.

This old man is ninety years old. That is a stick in his hand.

The baby is very young.
How old is he?
He is one year old.
The old man is very old.
How old is he?
He is ninety years old.

This box is four inches long and three inches wide and two inches high.

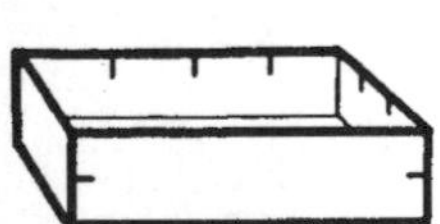

How long is it?
It is four inches long.

This room is twenty feet long and sixteen feet wide and twelve feet high.

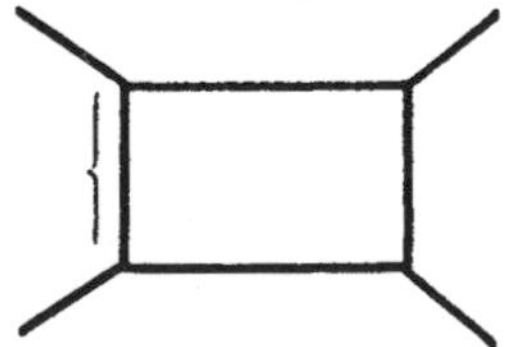

How high is the room?
It is twelve feet high.

This is a short coat.

This is a longer coat.

This is the longest coat of the three.

This is a thin book.

This is a thicker book.

This is the thickest book of the three.

This is a narrow street.

This is a wider street.

This is the widest street of the three.

Which is the narrowest street of the three?

This is a dirty face.

This is a cleaner face.

This is the cleanest face of the three.

Which is the dirtiest face?

Glass is harder than wood.

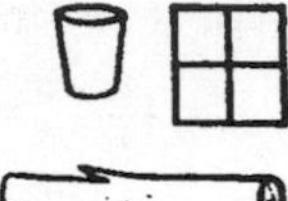

Wood is harder than bread.

Bread is harder than butter.

Which is the softest of these?
Which is the hardest?

This man is older than this boy.

The boy is older than this baby.

Which of them is the oldest?
The baby is the youngest.
He is very young.

This man is stronger than this boy.

The boy is not as strong as the man.

He is not as old as the man.

The baby is not as old as the boy or as strong as the boy.

This line

is as long as this line.

The two lines are equal (=).

This line is not as long as this line.

They are not equal.

A train may go one hundred (100) miles in an hour.

An airplane may go six hundred (600) miles in an hour.

Trains and airplanes are different sorts of transport.

What are some other sorts of transport?

Ships are another sort of transport.
How far may a quick ship go in an hour?
A quick ship may go thirty miles in an hour.

Automobiles and buses are other sorts of transport.

Airplanes, trains, ships, automobiles, buses and horses and carriages take us from one place to another.

We may go on our feet from one place to another.

When we go on our feet, we are walking.

Or we may go in a train or in a ship or in an automobile or in an airplane or on a horse or in a bus.

Some places are near to one another.

o o

Some places are far from one another.

o o

Places in Washington are near to one another.

The distance from one place to another is not far.

But some places in the United States are far from one another.

This is a map of North America.

These are mountains.

These are railroads.

These are roads.

These are rivers.

Men and women go up mountains. Mountains are high.

Trains go on railroads.

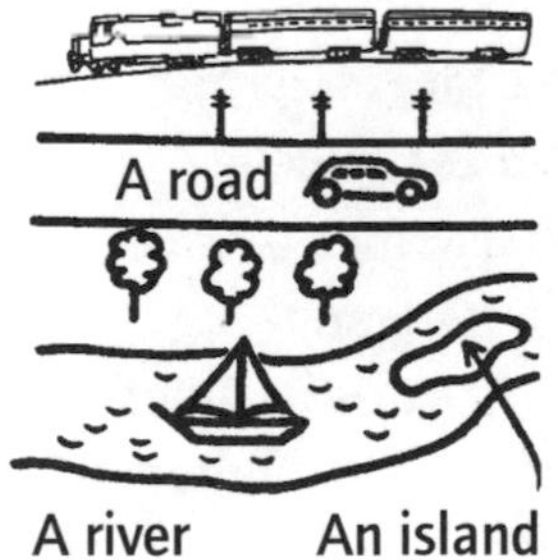

Ottawa, Washington, Mexico City, New York, and Los Angeles are towns.

This is a town.

The government of Canada is in Ottawa.

The government of the United States is in Washington.

The government of Mexico is in Mexico City.

How far is Ottawa from Mexico City?
The distance from Ottawa to Mexico City is about twenty-three hundred miles.
How far is New York from Los Angeles?
The distance between New York and Los Angeles is about twenty-five hundred miles.

How far is the mouth of the Mackenzie River from the mouth of the Mississippi?
The distance is about 3300 miles.
The mouth of a river is the place where it goes into the sea.

This is the earth. We are seeing it from the north.

There is more land than water on this side of the earth.

This is the earth. We are seeing it from the south.

There is more water than land on this side.

This is the moon.

The moon goes round the earth in a month.

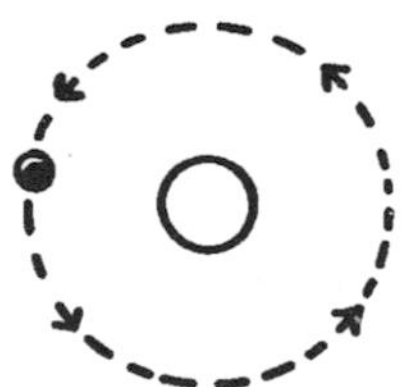

Do we ever see the other side of the moon?
No.

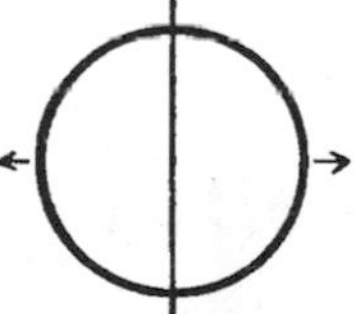

We see the same side of the moon at all times.
Why?

We see the same side at all times because the moon is turning round.

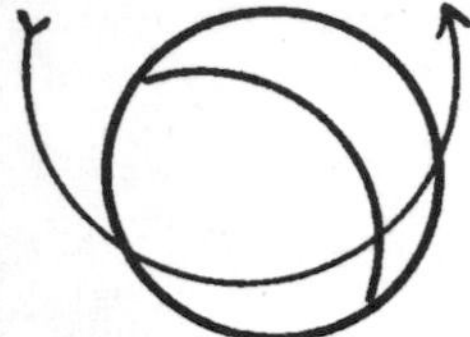

The moon

The earth

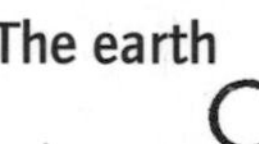

It is going round the earth and it is turning round itself.
It keeps the same side to the earth.

We see the same side of the moon at all times.
Sometimes we see it like this.

One half of the moon is dark.

The other half is bright.

This is a half moon.

Sometimes we see the moon like this.

This part of the moon is dark.

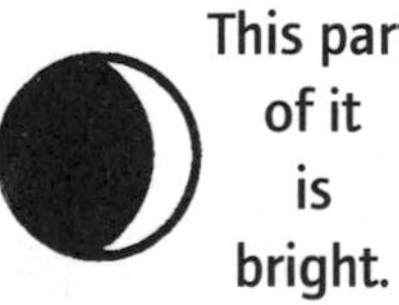

This part of it is bright.

This is a quarter moon.

Sometimes we see it like this.
This is a new moon.

This is a new hat.

This is an old hat.

And sometimes we see it like this.
This is a full moon.

This glass is full.

This glass is not full.

These are the changes of the moon.

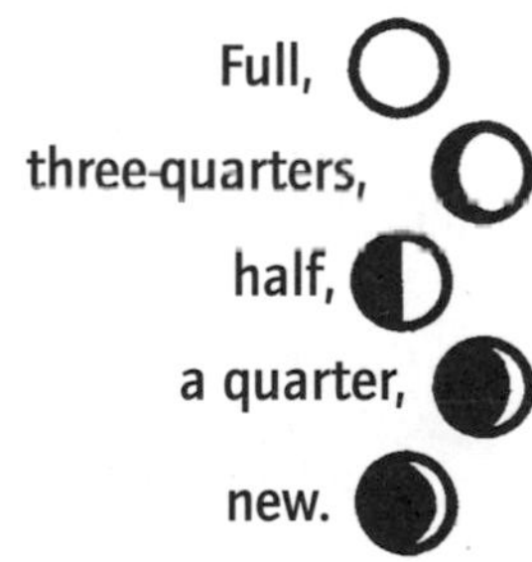

But at all times we see the same side of the moon.

Change? What is that?

Here is a change in the direction of this line.

And here is another change.

Here are two trains.
The man was in this train.
He is going to the other train.
He is making a change.
He is changing trains.

The potatoes were hard.

After a time they were soft.
There was a change in the potatoes.

This water was cold.

Now it is boiling.
That is a change.

There was a change in the water.

In the summer the leaves are on the trees.

In the fall the leaves come down off the trees.
That is a change.

I took a newspaper and gave a dollar ($1) to the man.

He took the dollar and he gave

a quarter (dollar)

and ten cents

and five cents.

This is the money which he gave to me with the paper.

The price of the paper was sixty cents. I got the paper and forty cents from him.

$1.00 -	100 cents
Paper -	60 cents
	40 cents

That money was my change.
I had a dollar.
After I got the paper
I had the paper and forty cents.
I did not have the dollar.
That was change.

QUESTIONS

a Is the boy nearer to the woman than the girl is?

Is the girl nearer to the boy than to the woman?

b Which of these two is farther from the tree?

Is the boy farther from the tree than from the girl?

c Which of these two glasses is full of water, the glass to the right or the glass to the left?

d Is there more land than water on the south side of the earth?

The answers are on page **74**.

a Which of these is a half moon, which is a full moon, which is a quarter moon, and which is a new moon?

b I got a book. I gave ten dollars to the man in the bookstore. He gave me the book and fifty cents. What was the price of the book? How much was the book? How much change did he give me?

c How far may a quick train go in an hour? How far may you go on your feet in an hour, four miles or forty?

d What are some different sorts of transport? Which is the quickest sort of transport?

The answers are on page **74**.

Page 72

- a No, the girl is nearer to the woman. Yes, the girl is nearer to the boy than to the woman.
- b The girl is farther from the tree. Yes, the boy is farther from the tree than from the girl.
- c The glass to the left is full of water.
- d No. There is more water than land on the south side of the earth.

Page 73

- a C is a half moon; B is a full moon; D is a quarter moon; and A is a new moon.
- b The price of the book was $9.50. It was $9.50. He gave me 50 cents change.
- c A quick train may go a hundred miles in an hour. I may go four miles but not forty.
- d Ships, trains, buses, and airplanes are different sorts of transport. The airplane is the quickest of these.

The distance through the earth from North to South is seven thousand nine hundred (7900) miles.

The distance round the earth is twenty-four thousand nine hundred (24,900) miles.

How far is the moon from the earth?
It is two hundred and forty thousand (240,000) miles from the earth.

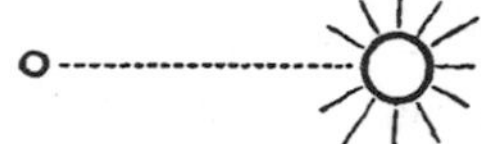

How far is the sun from the earth?
The distance of the sun from the earth is ninety-three million (93,000,000) miles.

What is that in your hand?
It is a ball.
The ball is small.

What is that in the sky?
It is the sun.
The sun is great.
The sun is a great ball of fire.

What is the size of the sun?
It is 864,000 miles through from one side to the other.

What is the size of the moon?
It is two thousand one hundred and sixty (2160) miles through from one side to the other.
Is the moon smaller than the earth?
Is the earth smaller than the sun?
Is the sun greater than the moon?

The moon is near the earth.
The earth is far from the sun.
New York is near Washington.
San Francisco is far from Washington.

New York
Washington
San Francisco

Are the stars smaller than the sun?
No. Some of the stars are much greater than the sun.
Are they nearer than the sun?
No, they are much farther than the sun.

How far from the earth is the nearest star?
It is over four light-years from the earth.
What is a light-year?
It is the distance which light goes in a year.

This is a flame.
It sends out light.

The sun sends out light.
The light goes out from the sun in every direction.

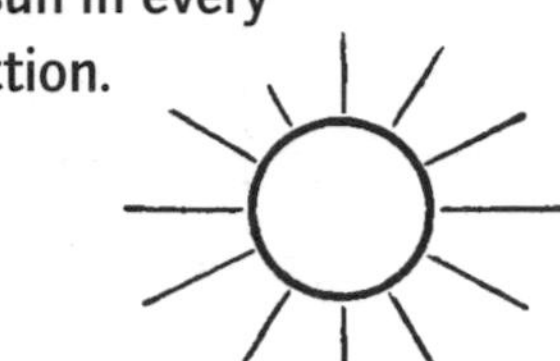

Light goes 186,300 miles in a second.
How far does it go in a year?

It goes about 6,000,000,000,000 miles in a year.

A light-year is 6,000,000,000,000 miles.

The nearest star is over four light-years from the earth.

The nearest star is 25,000,000,000,000 miles from the earth.
The nearest stars are very far from us.
Some of the stars are very much farther.
The farthest stars are thousands of light-years from us.

The sun sends its light out in every direction.

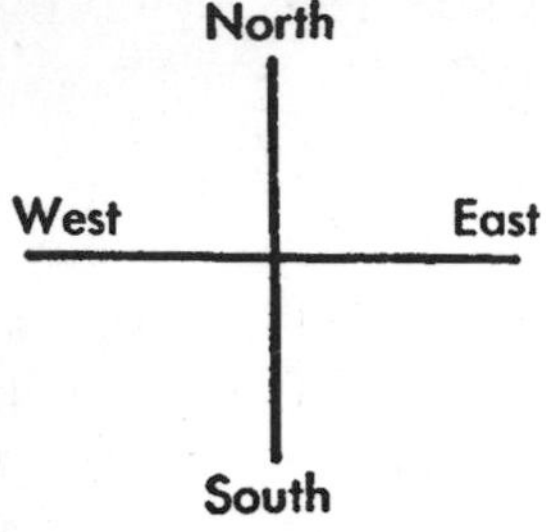

These are four directions.

Up and down are two other directions.

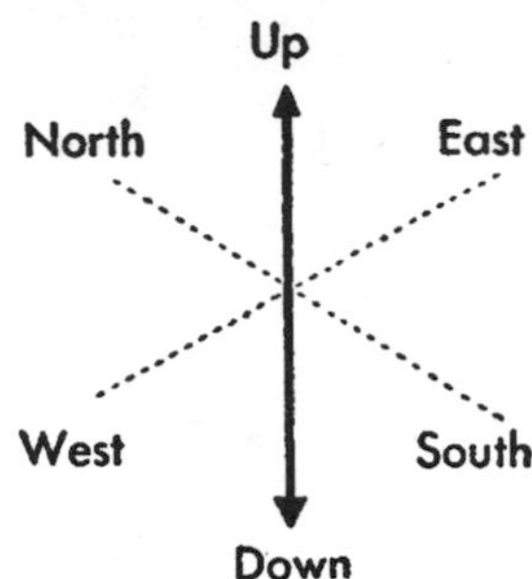

This boy has six apples in his hands.
He is on a branch of a tree.

He will send the six apples in different directions.

He sent one apple north, another apple south, another east, and another west.

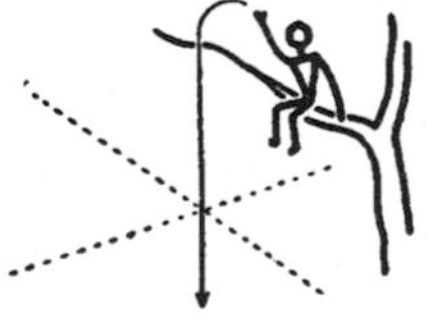

He sent another apple down.
He sent five apples in five directions.

He sent the last apple up.
But then it came down.
Why did it come down?

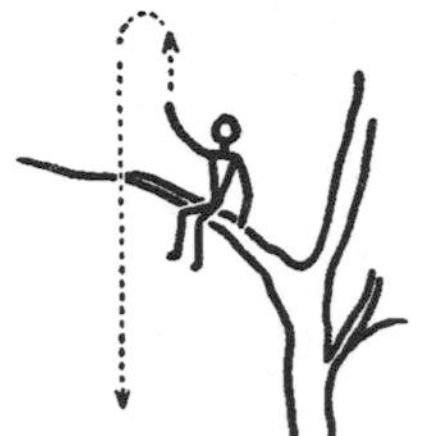

The first apple went north and then it came down. The other apples went south and east and west and then they all came down to the earth.

They all came down to the earth?
Why did they come down?

The first apple...
The last apple...
What is "the first"...?
What is "the last"...?

These men are in a line.
This is the first man.

This is the last man.

Here are three dogs.
Which is the first dog?
Which is the last dog?
The other dog is the dog in the middle.
He is between the first dog and the last dog.
Two of the dogs are white.
The other dog is black.
The dog in the middle is black.

Here are two bodies.
One is a great body.
It is the earth.
The other is a small body.
It is an apple.
The apple is coming down to the earth.
Why?

It is coming down because there is an attraction between the two bodies.
The attraction between them makes the apple come down.

All bodies which have weight have an attraction for one another.

Here are two bodies.
These are springs.

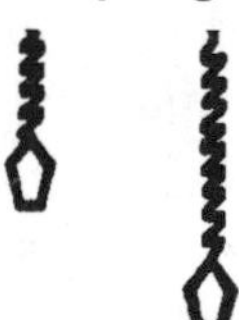

Which body has the greater weight?

Here are two men.

This man is thin.

His body is thin.

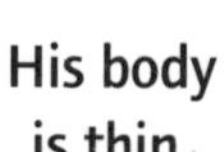

This man is fat.

His body is fat.

Which man's weight is greater?

This is a scale.

A scale is an instrument for measuring weight.

Which man's weight is greater?
They are on the scale.

The weight of the thin man is 100 pounds.

The weight of the fat man is 200 pounds.

Clocks are instruments for measuring time.

This is a watch.

Watches and clocks are instruments for measuring time.

This is an instrument for measuring heat.

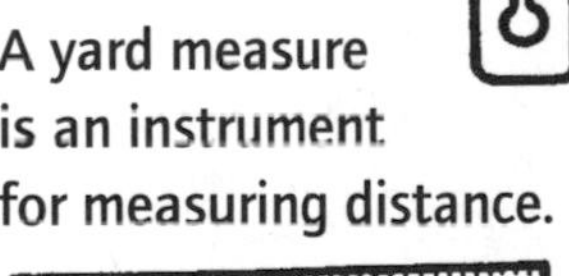

A yard measure is an instrument for measuring distance.

Inches, feet, yards, meters, and miles are measures of distance.

All bodies have an attraction for one another.

If the bodies are great the attraction between them is great.

If the bodies are small the attraction is small.

If the bodies go farther from one another the attraction gets smaller.

Distance	Attraction
1	1
2	1/4
3	1/9
4	1/16
5	1/25

Here is a light.

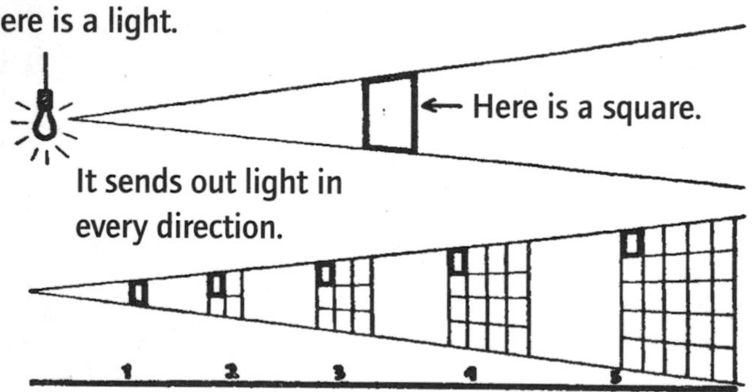

I put the square at different distances from the light. At distance 1, it gets all the light which is going out between the lines. At distance 2, it gets one-fourth of the light. At distance 5, it gets one twenty-fifth. It is the same with the attraction between bodies.

What keeps the moon up in the sky? Why does not the moon come down?

The moon is a great body.
Its weight is great.
The earth is a great body.
Its weight is eighty-one times the weight of the moon.
Two times three is six.
$2 \times 3 = 6$

The moon and the earth are not very far from one another.
The distance between them is about two hundred and thirty-nine thousand (239,000) miles.

Because they are great bodies and near one another, the attraction between the moon and the earth is very great.
Why does the moon not come down to the earth?
That is a question.

The answer is: "Because it is going round the earth."

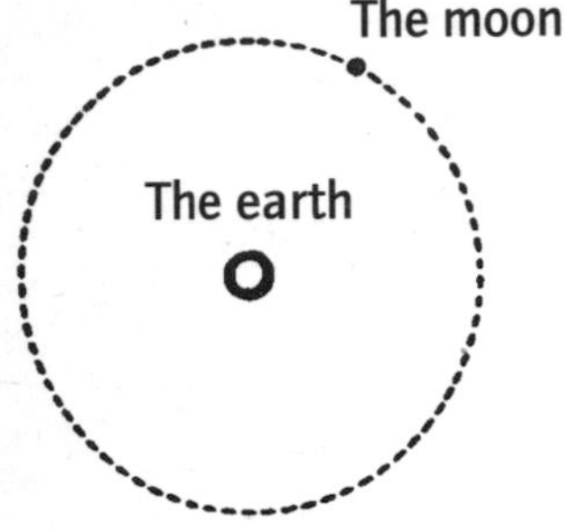

This is a cord in my hand. The cord has a weight at its end.

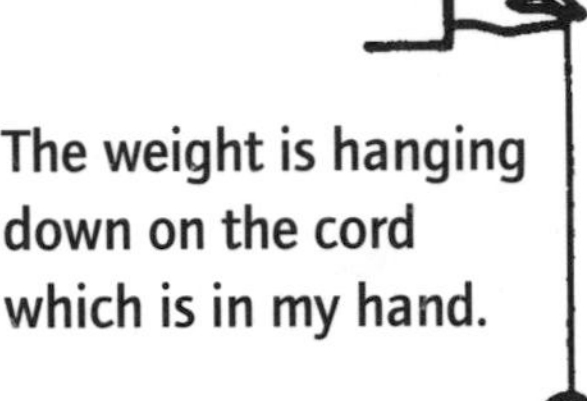

The weight is hanging down on the cord which is in my hand.

I make the weight go round on the cord.

I keep the end of the cord in my hand.

Now I let the end of the cord in my hand go.

The weight goes off in a straight line. It takes the cord with it.

The pull of the cord in my hand kept the weight from going off in a straight line.

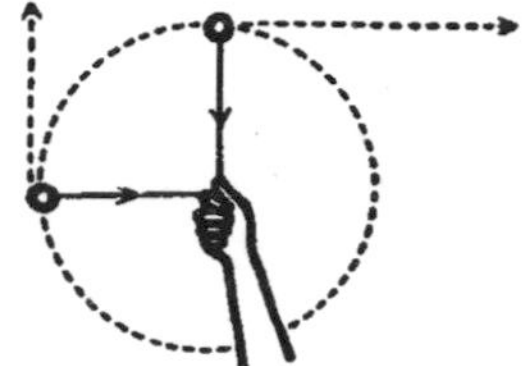

The attraction between the earth and the moon keeps the moon from going off in a straight line.

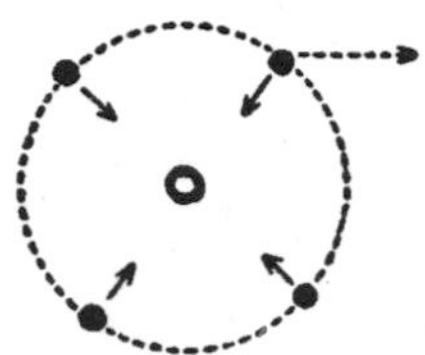

The moon goes round and round the earth... month after month.

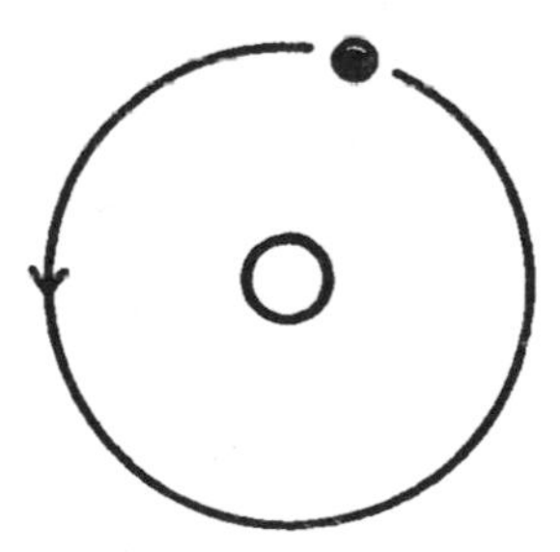

It does not get farther from the earth,

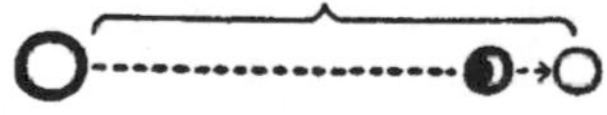

or nearer to the earth.

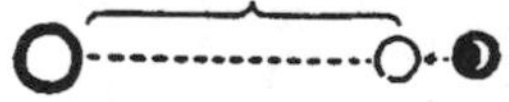

It keeps about the same distance from the earth.

Here is Sir Isaac Newton, the great man of science. Newton had a great mind.

He is under an apple tree.

It is the year 1666.

Those are apples which are over his head.

The seat has three legs.

Here is an apple which was over his head. The apple was on a branch of the tree.

The apple came off the branch. It came down.

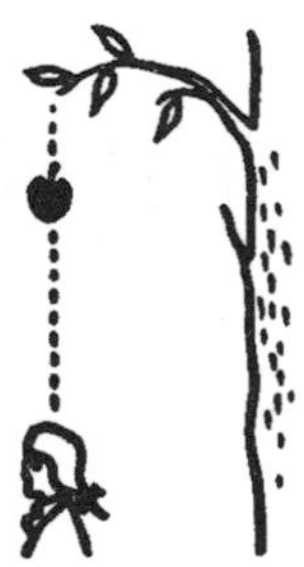

It came down on Newton's head.

That is the story.
The story may be true or it may not be true.

But that is the story. It comes from the great writer, Voltaire.

True?
2 + 2 = 4. That is true.
2 + 2 = 5. That is not true.
It is a false statement.
"Apples are fruit."
That statement is true.
"Apples are animals."
That statement is false.
False = not true
Short = not long
Shut = not open

In this story the fall of the apple on Newton's head was the cause of the idea.

The blow which the apple gave to Newton's head gave an idea to Newton.
It made a question come into Newton's mind.

This was the question:
"Have the fall of the apple and the motion of the moon the same cause?"

Here is a ball. It is hanging on a cord.

I will give a blow to the ball with this stick.

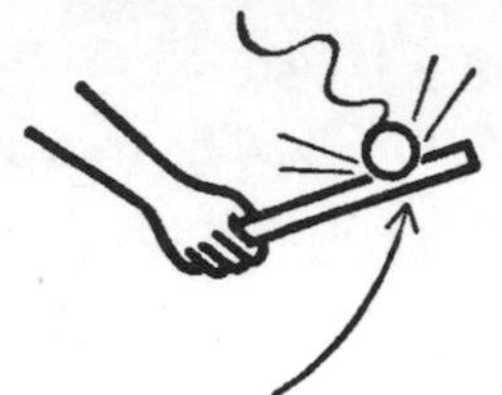

I gave the blow.
Now the ball is in motion.
What was the cause of the motion?
The blow of the stick was the cause of the motion.

The ball was not in motion before the blow. It was at rest. It was hanging on the end of the cord.

The blow was the cause of the motion.

After the blow the ball was in motion.
The motion came from the blow.
The motion was the effect of the blow.

Which of the statements on this page are true and which are false? Put a T before the true statements and an F before the false.

A 1 The earth is in motion.

2 The earth is turning round.

3 The earth goes round the moon.

B 1 The moon is greater than the sun.

2 The sun is colder than the moon.

3 The moon goes round the earth.

C 1 The attraction between two bodies gets greater as they go farther from one another.

2 The attraction between two bodies is greater when they are nearer.

3 When two great bodies are near one another the attraction between them is small.

D 1 When a blow puts a ball in motion, the blow is the cause of the motion.

2 When a blow puts a ball in motion, the motion is the effect of the blow.

3 When a body is in motion it is at rest.

The answers are on page **92**.

QUESTIONS

Milk comes from a cow. Heat comes from the sun, or a fire. Where do these things come from?

a potatoes	b cheese	c light
d letters	e flowers	f snow
g oranges	h meat	i eggs

Which of these things have a face?

a man	an icebox	a goat	a river
a dog	a clock	a bird	a table
a bone	a tree	an airplane	

Which of them have a mouth?
Which of them have hands?
Which of them have a door?

The answers are on page **92**.

QUESTIONS

a We put a bottle on a shelf.
Which of these things may we put on a shelf:
a book, a mountain, a cup, a box, a star, a clock, a horse, a distance, a plate, a bus, a river, a house, a spoon, a garden?

b We put potatoes in a pot.
Which of these things may we put in a pot:
water, windows, food, streets, tables, milk, soup, trains, salt, colors, eggs, wood, ideas?

c We put money in our pockets.
Which of these things may we put in our pockets:
pipes, education, letters, pencils, offices, islands, maps, hands, governments, buttons, watches, distance, balls, roofs, knives?

d We put our hats on.
Which of these things may we put on:
feet, boots, seats, gloves, shirts, walls, directions, coats, buildings, soap, scissors, collars, locks, socks, trousers, branches, trays, shoes, apples?

The answers are on page **92**.

Page 89

A 1 T	**B** 1 F	**C** 1 F	**D** 1 T
2 T	2 F	2 T	2 T
3 F	3 T	3 F	3 F

Page 90

a from the roots of a plant
b from milk
c from the sun or flames
d from persons
e from plants or from seeds
f from the sky or clouds
g from orange trees
h from animals
i from birds

A man, a dog, a clock, a goat, a bird may have a face.
A man, a dog, a goat, a bird, a river may have a mouth.
A man and a clock may have hands.
An icebox and an airplane may have a door.

Page 91

a a book, a cup, a box, a clock, a plate, a spoon.
b water, food, milk, soup, salt, eggs.
c pipes, letters, pencils, maps, hands, buttons, watches, balls, knives.
d boots, gloves, shirts, coats, collars, socks, trousers, shoes.

What is this?

The man has an umbrella
in his hand. It is open.
He has it over his head.
Why?

Because it is raining.
Water is coming down
from the sky.
The water is rain.
Rain is coming down.
Rain is falling.
It is raining.

The rain made the man
put up his umbrella.
That was the effect
of the rain.
Today is Monday.
Yesterday (Sunday)
the sun was bright.
There were no clouds in
the sky.

Today there are dark
clouds in the sky.
They come between us
and the sun.
The dark clouds keep the
light of the sun from us.

The rain comes down from the clouds on me. It comes down on my head.

The rain comes down from the clouds on us. It comes down on our heads.

Why is it raining today?
Yesterday the weather was good.
The sun was bright.
The air was warm.

Today the weather is bad.
The rain is coming down.
The wind is blowing.
It is cold and the rain makes us wet.

Tomorrow the weather may be worse.
It may be very cold.
All the water may be ice.
Snow may be coming down making everything white.
Will tomorrow be like this?
Is this winter or summer?

Or tomorrow the weather may be better.
The sun may be bright again.
The air may be warm again and the streets may be dry again.
Will tomorrow be like this?

What are the causes of these changes in the weather? Change? What is that? (See page 70.)

Here is a line.

Here is a change in the direction of the line.

What is the cause of these changes in the weather?

Good	Bad
Dry	Wet
Warm	Cold

Weather

Why are there these changes of weather?

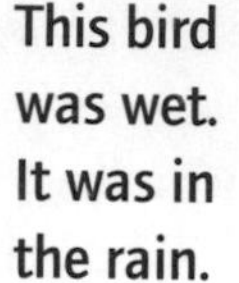

This bird was wet. It was in the rain.

Now it is dry.

That is a change. It was wet. It is dry.

There is not one cause only.
There are numbers of causes.
Changes in the heat which comes to us from the sun are one cause of changes of weather.

The amount of heat which the earth gets from the sun is different from time to time. There are changes in the sun.

If you take a look at the sun through a bit of dark glass you may see small marks on the face of the sun.

Amount? One dollar is a small amount of money. A million dollars is a great amount of money.

A drop of rain is a very small amount of water.

There is a small amount of water in this glass.

There is a great amount of water in the sea. This is the sea. Those are ships which are on the sea.

Changes in the heat which comes to the earth from the sun are one cause of changes in the weather.
This discovery is new.
A man of science made the discovery in 1944.

He made it by measuring the heat which comes to the earth every day from the sun.
The amount of heat is different from day to day.

On some days the sun sends more heat to the earth. On other days it sends less heat to the earth.

There is more water in this glass than in that.

More

Less

We are making new discoveries every day.
Columbus made the discovery of America in 1492.
Columbus came to America in his ship in 1492.

What were some other great discoveries?
One of them was fire.

Fire is of very great use to us. It gives us heat.

Another great discovery was the wheel.

Wheels are round.

They go round.

They are of very great use to us.

Another great discovery was clothing.

What are these?
These are some other sorts of clothing.

A skirt

A shirt

The making of cloth was a great discovery.
This is how we make cloth.

These are threads. (See page 47.)
They go across from one side to the other of a frame.

These are other threads. .

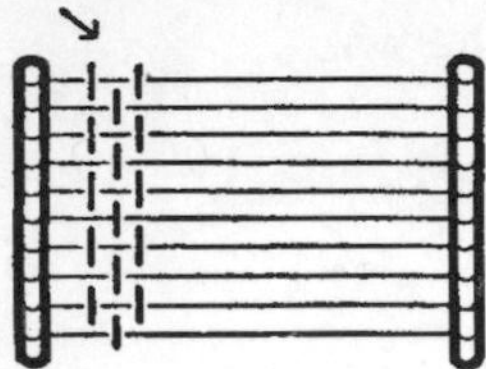

They go across the first threads.

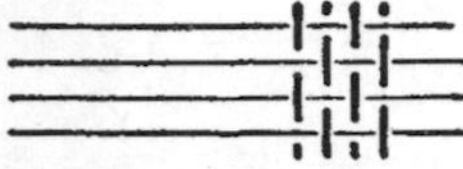

They go under and over them.

This is cloth.

This is a roll of cloth. We make clothing from cloth. We make cloth from threads.

We make threads from wool and cotton and silk.

We get wool from sheep.

Wool is the thick warm hair of sheep. We take the wool off the sheep's back with scissors.

We make threads from the wool by twisting the hairs round and round.

That wheel is going round.
It is giving a twist
to the thread.
It is twisting the
thread.

We get cotton from the cotton plant.

Cotton is the soft white hair round the seeds of the plant.

These are different sorts of seeds.

Plants come up from seeds which come from other plants of the same sort.

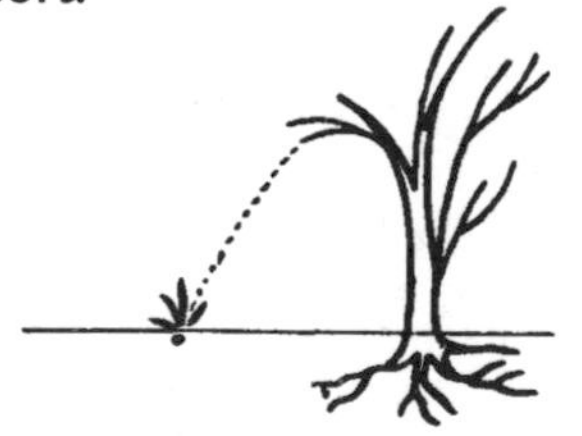

We get silk from the silkworm.

This worm makes a soft strong thread of silk and puts it round itself like a coat.

Wool, cotton, and silk are different sorts of cloth.
We make clothing of all these sorts of cloth.

When the weather is cold we put on thick warm wool clothing.
When the weather is warm we put on thin cotton clothing.
Cotton clothing is not as warm as wool clothing.

Thick clothing keeps us warm.
It keeps us warmer than thin clothing.
Thick cloth keeps air in it, between the threads.
The air does not let heat go through it.

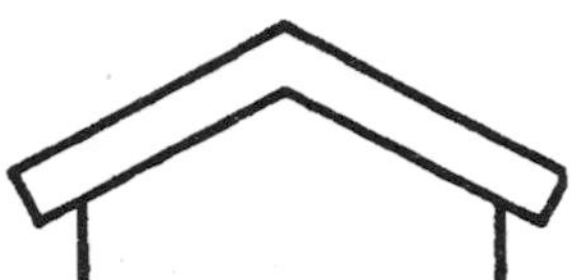

A thick roof keeps the heat of the house in.
A thin roof lets the heat go through it.

A thick roof keeps the heat of the sun out.

Here is a pencil.
It is straight.
It is not bent.

Here is a glass of water.

I put the pencil in the water.

The pencil seems bent where it goes into the water.

The pencil is straight but it seems bent.

It seems like this.

But it is like this.

It is straight, not bent.
It seems bent, not straight.

Before I put the pencil in the water it seemed straight.
It was straight.

After I put it in the water it seemed bent.
It wasn't bent.

When it is in the water it seems bent.

When it is out of the water we see that it is straight.

Why did it seem bent when it was in the water?

This is a light.
A light sends out light.
The light which it sends out goes in straight lines.

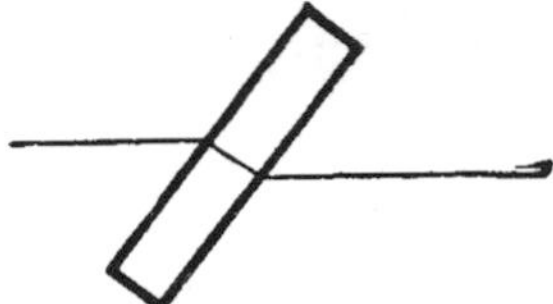

Here is a bit of glass.
A ray of light is going through the glass.

Where the light goes into the glass, it is bent.

It is bent again where it comes out of the glass into the air.

Here is your eye.

You are looking at the pencil in the glass of water.

The light from the pencil is bent where it comes out of the water into the air.

It is bent here.

The pencil is not bent. But the light from it is bent.

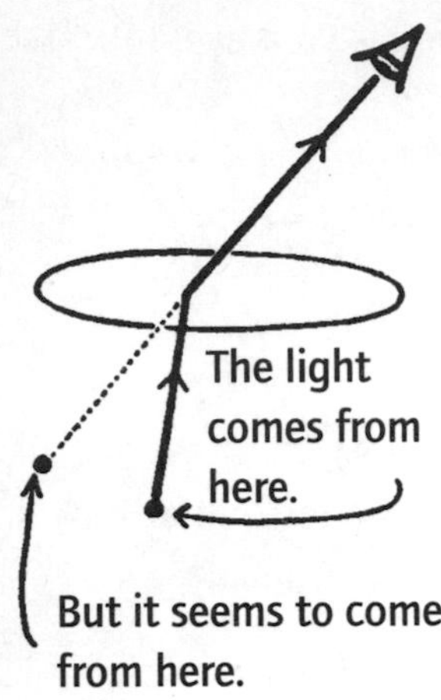
The light
comes from
here.
But it seems to come
from here.

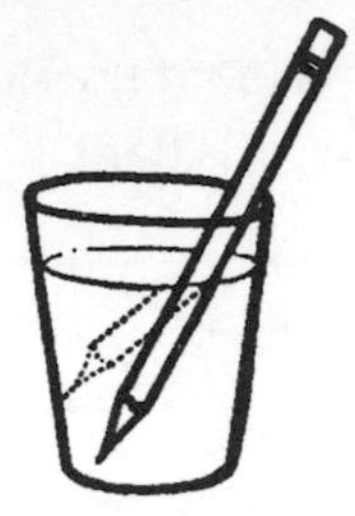
The part of the pencil
which is under the water
seems to be where it
is not.

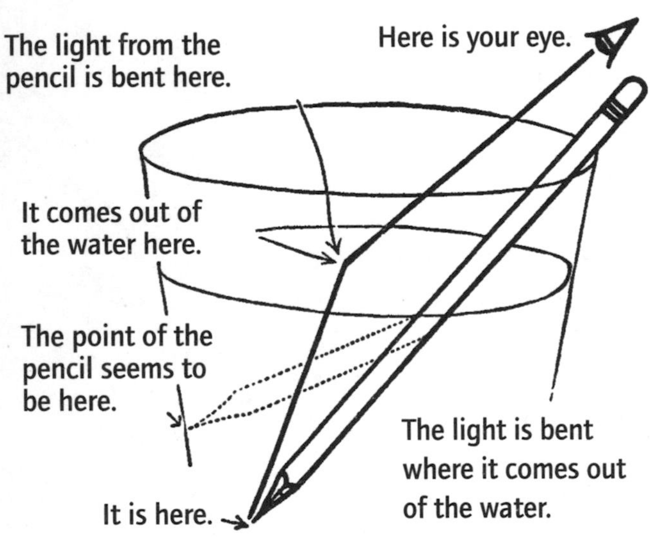
The light from the
pencil is bent here.
Here is your eye.
It comes out of
the water here.
The point of the
pencil seems to
be here.
It is here.
The light is bent
where it comes out
of the water.

This is a looking glass.

What do you see in the looking glass?
I see a girl's face in the glass.

She is looking at herself in the glass.
What does she see in the looking glass?
She sees herself in the glass.

She seems to be here.

She is on this side of the glass.
She seems to be on the other side of the glass.

Why? Because the glass sends the light back.

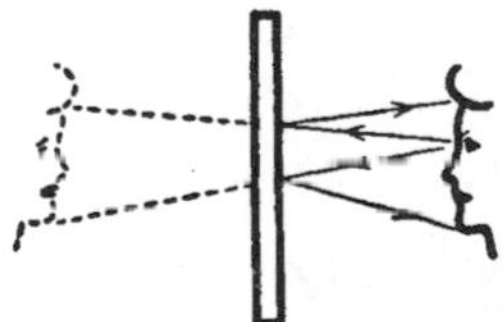

There seem to be two girls in this picture.
There is only one.

What is this man doing? He is working with a spade. That is his work.

What is this woman doing?

She is working with her needle. That is her work.

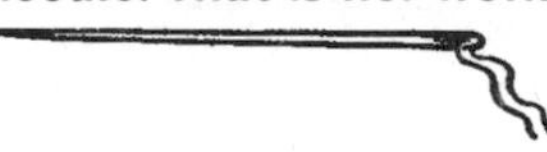

What is this man doing? He is making shoes. He is a shoemaker. That is his work.

These are shoes.

These are boots.

He makes boots and shoes. That is his work.

What is this man doing?
He is putting paint on the door.
He is painting the door.
He is a painter.
That is his work.

This is his paint.

This is his brush.

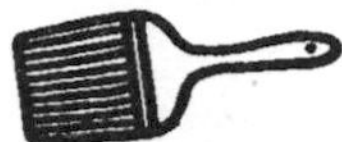

He puts the paint on with his paint brush.

2	3	14
2	7	26
4	10	40

This is addition.

The boy is doing addition.
That is his work.

This is a bank.

This is a check.

We keep money in banks. Banking is an important sort of business. Men and women in banks and business houses keep accounts.

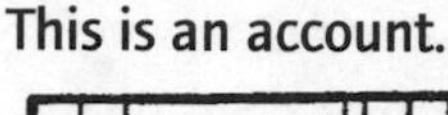
This is an account.

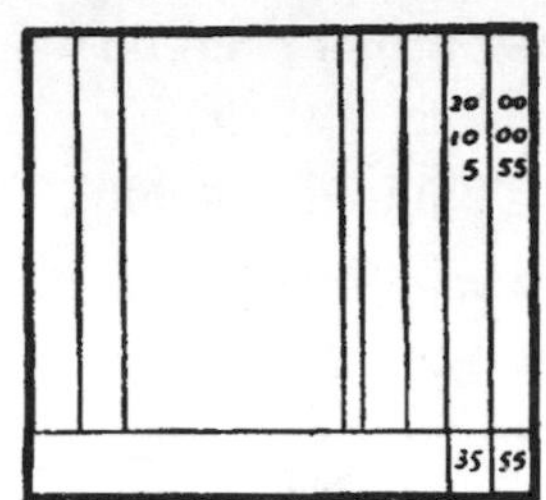

Keeping accounts is an important part of business.

Keeping accounts is one sort of work.

These are account books.

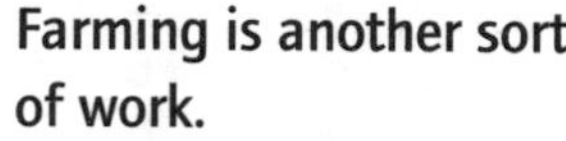
Farming is another sort of work.

This is a farm.

This is a cart.

This is a plow.

The plow is turning up the earth.

This is a field.

The farmer is plowing the field.
That is part of his work as a farmer.

The farmer has an account with his bank.
He puts his money in the bank.
He keeps money in the bank.
He gets money from the bank.

The account says how much money he has in the bank.
Farming and keeping accounts are two different sorts of work.

What sort of work is this man doing?
He is cutting wood.

What sort of work is this woman doing?
She is washing stockings and dresses.

What sort of work does this man do?
He keeps a store.

It is a fruit store.
He is a storekeeper.

What sort of work does this woman do?
She keeps a house.

It is her house.
She is a homemaker.

Put your fingers across one another like this.

I have my first and second fingers across one another.

Across?
These two lines go across one another.

My second finger is over and across my first finger.

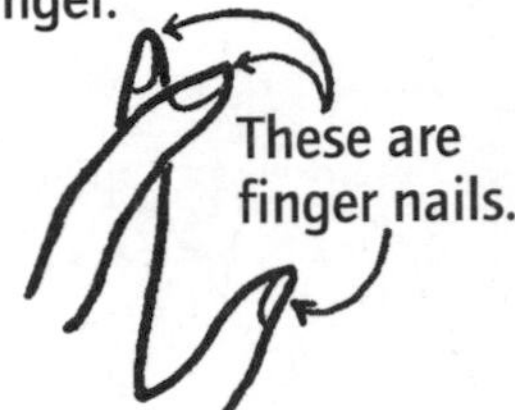

Did you put your fingers across one another?
That is right.
You have your fingers across one another.

Now take a pencil and give a touch to one finger, and then a touch to the other and then put the pencil between them. Do this with your eyes shut.

You will have a strange feeling.
Are two pencils touching your fingers, or is only one pencil touching them?

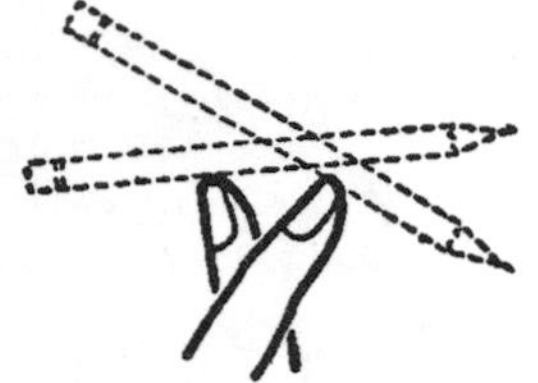

Do you have the strange feeling that two pencils are there?
When you are touching one finger only, you seem to be touching the other?

Why is that?
Here is the answer.

When the fingers are like this, or like this, they do their work together.

But when they are across one another they do not do their work together.
Then a touch to one sometimes seems to be a touch to the other.

What is their work?
What do the ends of our fingers do?
Their chief work is touching.

Those fingers are touching the cover of a book.
Touching gives us knowledge.
When our eyes are shut,

or when we are looking in another direction,
(She is touching the book)

or when we are not able to see, we get knowledge through touching and feeling with our fingers.

The chief work of the ends of our fingers is touching.
Here is a man who is not able to see.

That is a Braille book which he has before him.
He is reading the book with the ends of his fingers.

Braille letters and words are like this. He is touching them with the ends of his fingers.

This other man is reading with his eyes.
He is not reading with his fingers.

What are those things on his nose?
They are his glasses.

What is the work of the eyes?

Seeing. Their work is seeing.

What is the work of the ears?

Hearing. Their work is hearing.

Is talking or taking in food the chief work of the mouth?

What is the work of the legs?

Walking. Walking is their chief work.

What is the work of the mouth?

What is the work of the hands?
Taking things up, putting them down, getting things, giving things, making things.
We do things with our hands.

QUESTIONS

a Is there more water in the sea than in a river?

b Give the names of three great discoveries.

c What is wool?
What is cotton?
Where do we get silk from?

d Why is thick clothing warmer than thin clothing?

e What is the chief work of the eyes, the ears, the mouth, and the fingers?

f What sorts of transport go on wheels?

g Where does smoke come from? Where does steam come from?

h Where do we get wood from?

The answers are on page **120**.

QUESTIONS What are these things?

The answers are on page **120**.

Page 118

- a There is more water in the sea than in a river.
- b Fire, the wheel, and clothing were three great discoveries.
- c Wool is the hair of sheep.
  Cotton is the hair round the seeds of the cotton plant. We get silk from the silkworm.
- d Because thick clothing keeps heat from going through it.
- e The chief work of the eyes is seeing, of the ears is hearing, of the mouth is taking in food, and of the fingers is touching.
- f Carts, automobiles, and trains go on wheels.
- g Smoke comes from fire. Steam comes from boiling water.
- h We get wood from trees.

Page 119

- a a cart
- b a plow
- c a boot
- d a looking-glass
- e a skirt and a shirt
- f a wheel
- g a fire
- h a spade
- i a roll of cloth
- j an umbrella

Seeing and hearing and touch are three of our senses.
We get knowledge through our eyes (seeing), through our ears (hearing), and through our fingers (touching).
These are three of our chief senses.

Another sense is taste.

This is a man's tongue.

These are his lips.

This is his chin.

The chief work of the tongue is tasting.

Here is some white powder on a plate.
It may be salt or it may be sugar. Which is it-salt or sugar?

She is tasting the powder.
She has some of it on her finger.
She is putting some of the powder on her tongue.
She is tasting it.

We get salt from the sea.
The water in the sea has salt in it.

We get salt from salt mines.
Some mines are deep.
They go far down into the earth.

We get sugar from plants.
We get it from the stems of some plants.

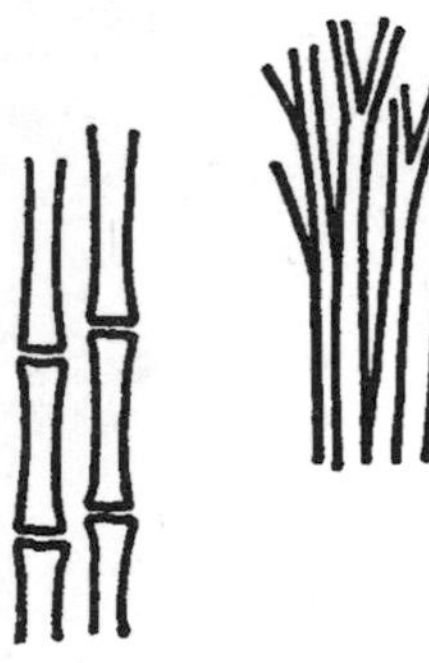

We get sugar from the roots of some plants.

The salt or sugar which we put in our food is a white powder.

The taste of sugar
is sweet.

This is a cake.

It has white sugar on
the top.
Cakes with sugar on
them are very sweet.

This is an orange.

This is its skin.

Some oranges are sweet.
But the taste of their skin
is bitter.

Salt has a salt taste.
Sugar has a sweet taste.
To the eye salt and sugar
seem the same.

But to the tongue they
are very different.

Salt

Their taste is
very different.

Sugar

What is the work of the nose?
What do we do with our noses?
She has a flower in her hand.
She is smelling the flower.

Some flowers have a sweet smell.
Some flowers have no smell.

This is grass.
These flowers are in a garden.
They have a sweet smell.

These are pigs.
Some pigs are dirty.
Some pigs are clean.
(See page 5.)
The smell of dirty pigs is not sweet.
It is a bad smell.

This is smoke.

This is a fire.

Some smoke has a good smell.
The smell may not be sweet, but it may be a good smell.
He is smoking a pipe.
Is the smell of the smoke good?

We see things with our eyes and we see their colors.
Here are some names of colors:

green red
blue yellow
white gray

What is the color of grass and leaves in spring?
Grass and leaves in spring are green.
What is the color of this girl's lips?
Her lips are red.

The sky is blue.

It is blue when it is clear.
The color of some clouds is white.
Other clouds are gray.

The sun is yellow.

Sometimes when it is going down

or coming up it is red.

This flame is yellow..

We see things with our eyes.
We see the sizes and colors of things.
Sometimes things seem to our eyes greater or smaller than they are.
They are not what they seem.

This man is tall. 

 This man is short.

This is a tall woman. 

 This is a short woman.

Here are two men.
Do they seem the same size?

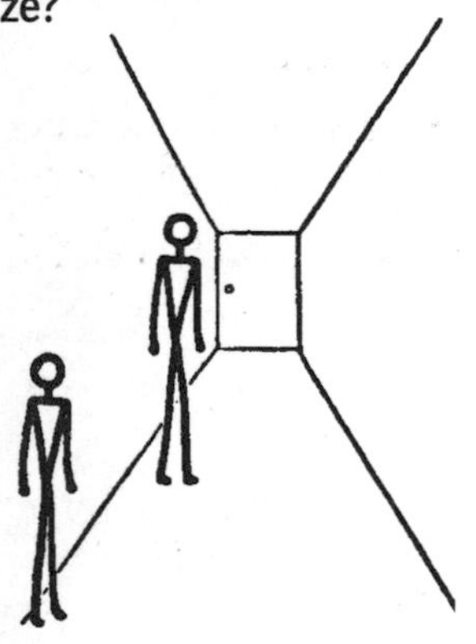

Which of them seems taller?
Does the man who is farther seem taller than the man who is nearer?
The pictures of them are the same size.
The lines in the picture make the man who is nearer seem shorter.

Seeing, hearing, touch, taste, and smell are "the five senses."
But we have more than five senses.
Which are some of the other senses?

Our sense of how warm or how cold things are is another.
Here is some cold water with ice in it.
It is very cold.

Here is some water in a kettle.
The water is boiling.
Steam is coming out of the kettle.

Here are three basins.
The basin to the right has very warm water in it.
The basin to the left has cold water in it.
The basin in the middle has water which is not cold and not warm in it.

I put my hands in the basins at the sides.
One of my hands is in the cold water; the other is in the warm water.
I keep them there for a time.

Now I am putting them together into the middle basin where the water is not cold and not warm.

What is this?
This water seems warm to one hand and it seems cold to the other!
It is the same water.
But it seems cold and warm at the same time!

Why is this?
It is because one hand was in warm water and the other in cold water before I put them in this middle basin.

Another sense is our sense of motion.
Here is a seat which goes round and round.

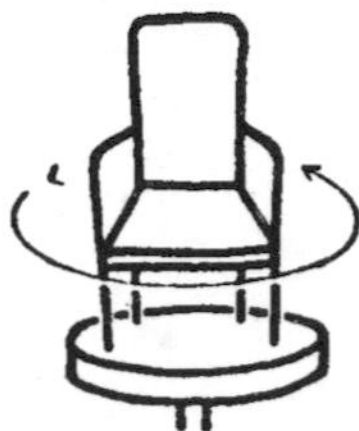

A man is in the seat.
He is going round and round...

At first he has a feeling that he is in motion.
He has the feeling that he is going round.
The seat, with the man in it, keeps on turning round at the same rate.
It does not go quicker.
It does not go slower.

After a time the man has a feeling that he is not in motion.
But there is no change in the rate at which the seat is turning.
It is going round the same number of times a minute.

After a time, if the rate of turning is the same, the man seems to himself to be at rest (not in motion).

He is like all the men and women on the earth. We are all turning round all the time with the earth, but we seem to ourselves to be at rest.

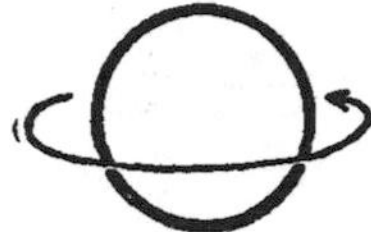

We have no feeling that we are in motion.
This is because the rate of turning is the same.
The man is in motion.
He seems to himself to be at rest.

Here are three boys and a dog.
Two of the boys are taking a rest.
They are resting on their beds.
The other boy and the dog are in motion.

Now, put a stop to the motion of the seat.
When you do that the seat is at rest.
The man is not in motion.

But he has a feeling that he is turning round and round.
This is a picture of his feelings.

He is not turning round.
But he seems to himself to be turning round.
And everything round him seems to be turning round.
Why is this?

It is because change in our motion is the cause of our feelings of motion.
Through our sense of motion we get knowledge of changes in the rate and direction of our motion.

What is he doing?
He is hammering.

This is his hammer.

These are nails of different sizes.

He is putting the cover on a box.
He is nailing down the cover of the box.
The cover is on the top of the box.

The blows of the hammer make a noise.
He is making a very loud noise.

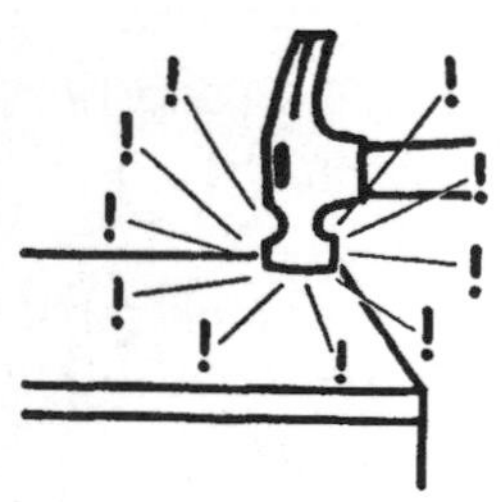

Mary has her hands over her ears.
"What a noise!" She is saying, "What a noise you are making."

Some noises are loud.
These are guns.

Guns make loud noises.
Those guns make more noise than this gun.

What is this?

It is a whistle.
It is a steam whistle.
It is making a loud noise.

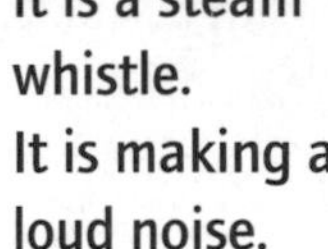

This boy has a pocket whistle.

He is making some noise with it but not much noise.

This is music.

This is a song.

These are notes.

This is a high note.

This is a low note.

This is a very high mountain.

These are high mountains.

This is a high building.
It is a church.

This is a low building.

Noises and songs
are sounds.
What are sounds?
They are the effects of
waves in the air.

These
are waves in the sea.

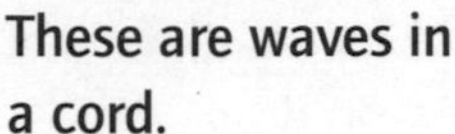

These are waves in
a cord.
One end of the cord is
fixed to a tree and the
boy has the other end.
He is shaking it up
and down.

With every shake he
sends a wave down the
cord to the tree.

As the wave goes down
the cord this part, which
was up,

goes down.
And this part,
which was down,
goes up.

These are waves in the air.
They come to our ears.
They have effects in our ears and brains.
Those effects are sounds.

Here is a brain.
The part of the brain which does the most work in hearing has the word HEARING on it.

"The most"?
Some things have water in them.

This cup has some water in it.

This bucket has more water in it.

The sea has the most water in it.

Some animals have brains:
a horse has some brains;
a monkey has more brains;
and a person has the most brains of the three.

I have two dollars.
You have twenty dollars.
He has a thousand dollars.
He has more money than we have.
You have more than I have.
He has the most money.

I have less money than he has.
I have less than you have.
I have the least money.

The most	$1000	
More	$20	less
	$2	The least

This is the highest note.

This is a lower note,

but it is higher than this note.

Which is the lowest note of the three?

Farming is an important sort of work.

Is it more important than banking?

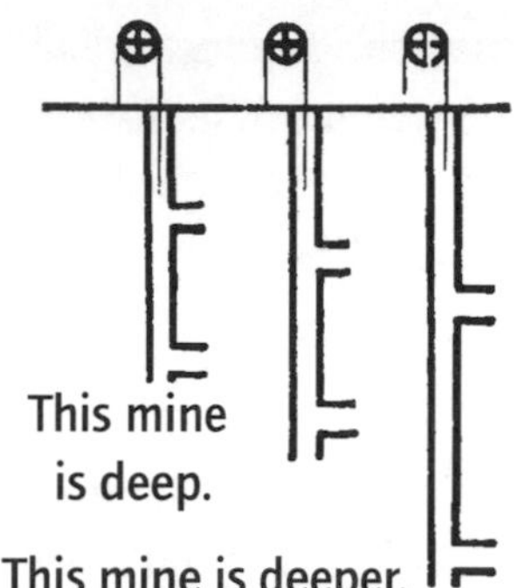

This mine is deep.

This mine is deeper.

This mine is the deepest of the three.

This plate has some salt on it.

This plate has more salt on it.

This plate has the most salt on it.

It has more salt on it than the other plates.

This is a good book.

These are two other good books.

One of them is better than the others. It is the best book of the three.

This is a bad fire.

This is a worse fire.

This is the worst fire of the three.

She is looking at herself in a looking glass. Again and again, every day, she takes a look at herself in a glass.

Whenever she sees a looking glass she goes to it and takes a look at herself.

Why?

Because looking at herself in the glass gives her pleasure.
She is beautiful.
She sees that she is beautiful.

Looking at himself in the glass gives him no pleasure.
It gives him pain. Why?
He sees himself.
Is he beautiful?

"Pleasure?" What is that?
"Pain?"What is that?

Put your finger
in the flame.
No, I will not.
Why not?
Because of the pain.

Here is a nail.

You put your
finger nail
over this
nail, and I
will give it
a blow with
this hammer.

No, you will not.
I see what pain is now.
I see what the sense of the
word "pain" is now.
This is another use of the
word "sense."

That is pain.
Pleasure is the opposite
of pain.
"Opposite?" Good is the
opposite of bad.

Good weather.
The day is bright.
The air is warm.
The sky is blue.
They are happy.

Bad weather.
The wind is blowing.
The rain is falling.
It is cold. It is wet.
They are unhappy.

Bright is the opposite of dark.

Warm is the opposite of cold.

White is the opposite of black.

What is the opposite of dry? (See page 8.)
What is the opposite of happy?

Which of these is
a high building?
What is the other?

What is the opposite
of narrow?
Is this street narrow?

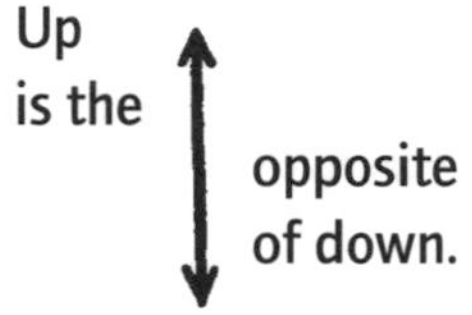

Up
is the
opposite
of down.

In is the opposite of out.

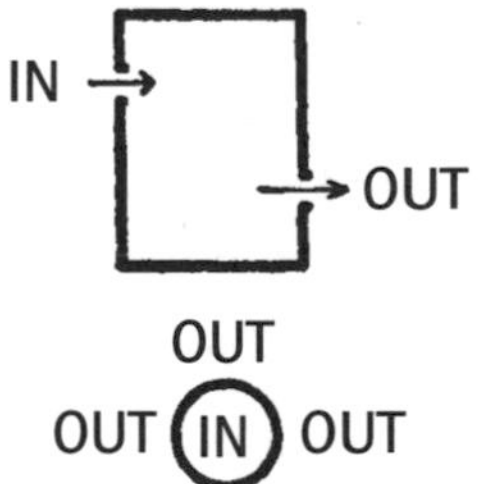

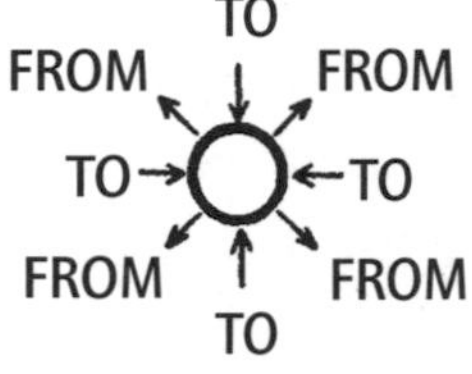

To is the opposite
of from.

Pleasure is the opposite
of pain.

Beautiful things give us pleasure.

When she sees herself in the glass, she sees that she is beautiful.
That gives her pleasure.

When I say that she is beautiful, that gives her pleasure.

There is a smile on her face now.

Why is the smile there?

It is there because she has a feeling of pleasure.
Her pleasure is the cause of her smile.
She is saying to herself, "I am beautiful."

She is saying to herself that she is beautiful.

A smile does not make a sound.
A laugh makes a sound.

A laugh is a smile with a sound.

This is a great painting by Leonardo.

Its name is the Mona Lisa.

The picture is beautiful. That is certain.

Was the woman beautiful?
Was Lisa herself beautiful?
That is not certain.

I have my idea of that.

He has his idea.

She had her idea.
We may have different ideas of how beautiful that woman was.
There is no measure of the beautiful.

She may or may not be beautiful.
But it is certain that she has a smile on her lips.
That is certain.

It is not certain that she is beautiful.

2 + 2 = 4. Two and two are equal to four. That is certain.

2 + 2 = 5. Two and two are not equal to five.
That is certain.

It is certain that 2 + 2 = 4.

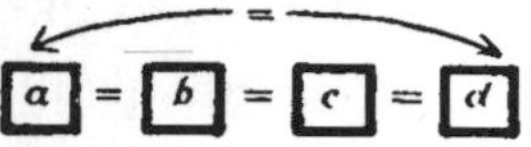

a is equal to *b*, and *b* is equal to *c*, and *c* is equal to *d*.
So *a* is equal to *d*.
Things which are equal to the same things are equal to one another.

Things which are like one another may be equal or they may not.

These two are like one another but they are not equal.

A smile is like a laugh.
But a laugh makes
a sound.

This girl is laughing.
She is happy.

She has a fall.
She gives a cry.

Now she is crying.
She is not laughing now.
She is crying. Why?

Because she gave her
knee a blow in her fall.

This is →
her knee.

She was on
her feet.

Then she was on
her face.
She had a fall.

The fall was the cause of
the blow to her knee.

The blow was the cause
of the pain in her knee.

And the pain in
her knee was the cause
of her crying.

Pleasure and pain
are feelings.
We have feelings of
pleasure and pain.
Here are some pleasures.

He is on the sand at the seaside, looking at and hearing the sound of the waves and warming himself in the sun.
These are pleasures.

Now he is taking a swim in the sea.

He is swimming through the waves.
He is a good swimmer.
To a good swimmer, swimming is a pleasure.

Now he is resting in the sun again after his swim.

After the water the sun on his skin is a pleasure to him.

Pleasure and pain are feelings.

When we put our fingers on things we have feelings—feelings of touch or of heat and cold.
But this is another use of the word "feeling."

The man is feeling the bit of wood with his fingers. Is it rough or is it smooth?

This is rough.

This is smooth.

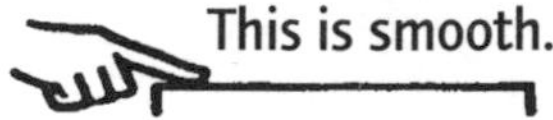

Things which give us pleasure have an attraction for us.
But it is not the same sort of attraction as the attraction between the earth and the moon.
(See pages 82-83.)

Our feeling of this attraction is named "desire."
When we have pleasure we have a desire for the pleasure to go on and go on...
Time goes on. The hands of the clock go on. Our feelings may or may not go on.

Some desires are stronger than others.
This baby sees the cat and he sees his ball.

The cat has an attraction for him.
He has a desire for the cat.

His ball has an attraction for him.
He has a desire for the ball.

Which will he go to?
If his desire for the cat is stronger than his desire for the ball, he will go to the cat.

He went to the cat.
His desire for the cat was stronger.

All our desires are for things which seem good to us.
They may not be good.
Our ideas of them may be wrong.

We get knowledge by putting questions. That is one way of getting knowledge. The answers may give us knowledge or they may not.

When the answers are right, they give us knowledge. When they are wrong they do not give us knowledge.

2 + 2 = 4 Right

2 + 2 = 5 Wrong

How far is the sun from the earth? Which is the right answer: "It is two miles away" or "it is much more than two miles away?" Which is the wrong answer to the question?

Which is his right hand?

Which is his left hand? He is facing you.

Now he has his back to you.

Which is his left hand now, and which is his right?

Our senses–seeing, hearing, touching, tasting, and smelling–are ways through which we get knowledge. Our ideas come to us through our senses.

This is a doorway.

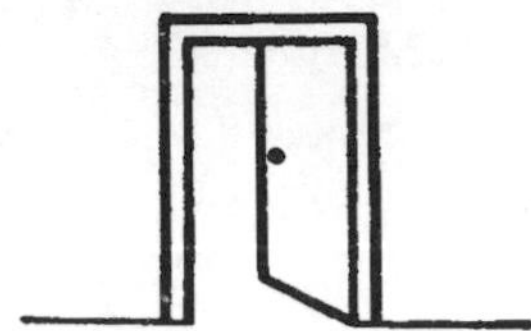

The way into the room is through the door. The way out of the room is through the door.

"Which is the way to the station?" "Take the first street to the right."

This man had no knowledge of the way to the station. Now he has the knowledge.

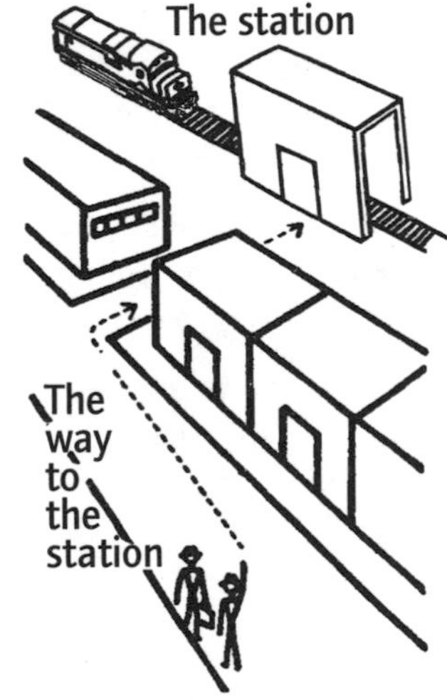

We get knowledge in different ways–through our senses,

through talk with others,

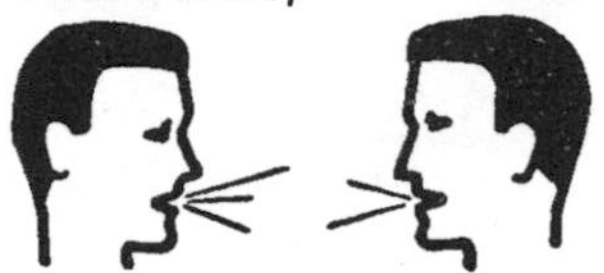

through the work we do with our hands and our heads, and through books.

These are all ways of getting knowledge.

Knowledge is very important.
It is important in itself.
And it is important as a way to other things.
A person who has no knowledge is of no use to others.

Is the word "use" part of your knowledge of English?
(See page 99.)
Knowledge gives us light. It makes things clearer to us.

This is a boy.

He will be a man.

He was a baby.

He seems to be about twelve years old now.

Every night he has a long sleep in his bed.

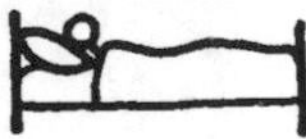

He goes to bed at eight every night.

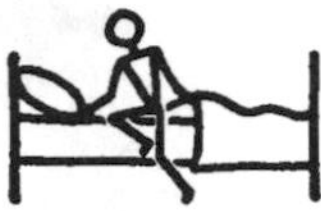

He gets up every morning at seven.

He gets out of bed and gives himself a good wash.

He puts his clothing on.

He says "Good morning" to his mother and father and takes his place at the table.

At school he sees his friends and does his work.

He keeps his thoughts on his work.

He does not let his thoughts go off to other things.

At play after school he sends the ball a long way.

He makes it go a long way.

Then he comes back from school.

Here he is with the family again.

Men and women
are persons.
They have their work.
They put and
take things,
and give
and get them.
They come
and go.

They see and
say things,
keep things,
and let them (go),
make and
send them.

Some seem happier than others.
All these sorts of things are done by men and women.
Things are put and taken by them.
Things are given and got by them.
Things are seen and said by them.
Things are kept and let go by them.
Things are made and sent by them.

Eve saw the apple.

She took it.

She gave it to Adam.
Eve did these things.

The apple was seen
by her.
It was taken by her.
It was given by her
to Adam.
These things were done
by Eve.

We may say this in
two ways.
She saw the apple
and took it and gave
it to Adam.

This may be said in
two ways.
The apple was seen by
Eve, and taken and given
by her to Adam.

I will do it.	It will be done by me.
I am doing it.	It is being done by me.
I did it.	It was done by me.
They will see it.	It will be seen by them.
They are taking it.	It is being taken by them.
They gave it.	It was given by them.
DO TAKE	DONE TAKEN
SEE GIVE	SEEN GIVEN

I will say it.	It will be said by me.
I said it.	It was said by me.
I made it.	It was made by me.
I kept it.	It was kept by me.
I let it go.	It was let go by me.
I put it there.	It was put there by me.
I got it.	It was got by me.
I sent it.	It was sent by me.
SAY MAKE KEEP	SAID MADE KEPT
LET PUT	LET PUT
GET SEND	GOT SENT

Every statement or question in this book has one or more of these sixteen words in it:

be	come	give	make
have	go	get	send
do	put	keep	see
seem	take	let	say

The first of these words, BE, comes into more statements than any other.
Here it is. It goes like this:

	Past	*Present*	*Future*
I	was	am	will be
He She It	was	is	will be
We You They	were	are	will be

Here are the other fifteen words. They go like this:

	Past	*Present*	*Future*
	had	have	will have
I	did	do	will do
	seemed	seem	will seem
	came	come	will come
	went	go	will go
We	put	put	will put
	took	take	will take
	gave	give	will give
	got	get	will get
You	kept	keep	will keep
	let	let	will let
	made	make	will make
	sent	send	will send
They	saw	see	will see
	said	say	will say

	Past	*Present*	*Future*
	had	has	will have
	did	does	will do
He	seemed	seems	will seem
	came	comes	will come
	went	goes	will go
	put	puts	will put
	took	takes	will take
She	gave	gives	will give
	got	gets	will get
	kept	keeps	will keep
It	let	lets	will let
	made	makes	will make
	sent	sends	will send
	saw	sees	will see
	said	says	will say

In English we do not make statements like this:

She gave you money to I. That is wrong.

We make statements like this:

She gave your money to me. That is right.

I	my	me	we	our	us
you	your	you	you	your	you
he	his	him			
she	her	her	they	their	them
it	its	it			

In English we make COMPARISONS like this:

good	better	best
bad	worse	worst
much	more	most
little	less	least
beautiful	more beautiful	most beautiful
small	smaller	smallest
bright	brighter	brightest
short	shorter	shortest
thin	thinner	thinnest

In English we make changes in names like this:

1 cat (dog, boot, day, nose, face...)	2 or more cats (dogs, boots days, noses, faces...)
1 glass (watch, brush...)	2 glasses (watches, brushes...)
1 body (cry, baby...)	2 bodies (cries, babies...)
1 knife (leaf, shelf...)	2 knives (leaves, shelves...)
1 tooth, foot	2 teeth, feet
1 man, woman	2 men, women

1 or more sheep, scissors, trousers

A SECOND WORKBOOK OF ENGLISH

Pages **2-11**

1 What is she doing?

She is putting a hairpin in her hair.

2 What is he doing?

3 What is she doing?

4 What are they doing?

5 What is he doing?

Pages **2-11**

1 **What sort of room is the woman in?**

She is in a bedroom.

2 **Where is the bag?**

3 **What is in the woman's left hand?**

4 **What does the woman see in the sock?**

5 **What is by the basin?**

6 Where are the trousers?

____

____

7 Where is the basin?

____

____

8 Where is the hairbrush?

____

____

9 Where are the shirts?

____

____

10 Where are the shoes?

____

____

Pages **17-18**

A Journey

Mr. and Mrs. James Grant and their son, Peter, are going on a journey from New York City in New York State to Salt Lake City in Utah. Some time before the journey Mr. Grant said to Mrs. Grant and Peter, "We will go by plane. A plane journey to Salt Lake City takes a very short time."

Peter said to his father, "There are horses and cows and sheep and pigs between here and Utah, aren't there? Do you see them from a plane?"

"No," said his father, "the plane goes very high in the air."

Mrs. Grant said, "Going by bus or train, you see all the states between New York and Utah and houses and men and women and boys and girls and animals."

Pages **17-18**

"You are right," said Mr. Grant. "You do see all these things. But it takes a long time to go by bus or train."

"Mother goes on a bus," said Peter, "when she goes to the store."

"But that is a short journey," his father said. "This will be a long one."

"We took a train when we went to Washington, D.C.," said Peter. "When we were there, you took a picture of me and mother in front of the White House, and a dog came and got in the picture with us."

"'Mother and me,' not 'me and mother,' Peter,"said his father.

"Yes, you did make a long journey by train when you were five," Mrs. Grant said. "And now is the time for another. My sister and her family are in Chicago. They are in a new house and have a new baby. We will go and see them. Then we will go to Salt Lake City."

"All right," Mr. Grant said. "We will make our journey in two parts. We will take a plane to Chicago and see your sister's family. Then we will take the bus which goes from there to Salt Lake City."

"Oh good!" said Peter. "We will go by plane and by bus!"

THIS IS A CAMERA.
WE TAKE PICTURES
WITH IT.

Pages **2-11**

when **front** **after** **train** **by** **going**
journey **before** **between**

1 The Grants are __going__ from New York City to Salt Lake City.

2 They will go ________ plane from New York City to Chicago.

3 Peter went on a long journey by ________ with his family when he was five.

4 Mr. Grant took a picture of Peter and his mother in ________ of the White House.

5 The ________ from New York City by plane takes a short time.

6 Illinois and Nebraska are two of the states ________ New York and Utah.

7 The Grants will go to Chicago ________ they go to Salt Lake City.

8 They will go to Salt Lake City ________ they see Mrs. Grant's sister in Chicago.

When the Grants were going to their plane, the wind took Mrs. Grant's hat off her head and up into the air. The hat came down by the side of a building. Mr. Grant went after it. In a short time he came back with the hat. "It is dirty and a bit wet," he said.

"Do I see a hole in the hat?" said Mrs. Grant.

"Where?" said Mr. Grant.

"Here," Mrs. Grant said, putting her finger on the hat. "Oh, I see now. It is dirty, but there is no hole."

Mr. Grant gave the hat to Mrs. Grant, saying, "Our plane is here. We have to get on it now. The hat will be dry in a short time." He took up two of the bags. Mrs. Grant had her hat and another bag in her right hand. Peter put his hand in her left hand, and they went over to the plane.

After they were in their seats and the plane was in the air, Mrs. Grant went to the washroom at the back of the plane with her hat and her bag. She put the hat, which was drying, and the bag to one side. Some of her hairpins were coming out of her hair. She took the other hairpins out, and her hair came down. She took her comb

and hairbrush out of the bag. After brushing and combing her hair, she put it up again with the hairpins. She put the comb and hairbrush back in her bag and then took out another bag in which she had her washcloth. She had no soap with her, but there was some soap in the washroom. She put the washcloth in the warm water in the basin and put soap on it. After washing her face and hands, she put the washcloth in the washcloth bag again. When the wet washcloth was in its bag, it did not make her other things wet.

By this time Mrs. Grant's hat was dry. It was a cloth hat. She took a brush and gave the hat a good brushing. In a short time the dirty part of the hat was clean again.

Pages **2-11**

plane basin soap bags cloth dry washing

drying brushing combing dirty hole wet

clean washcloth comb hairpins brush

1 The Grants got on a ______________ in New York city.

2 They had three ______________ with them.

3 Mrs. Grant's hat was a ______________ hat.

4 Before the wind took Mrs. Grant's hat off her head, her hat was ______________ and ________________ .

5 After the wind took her hat off, it was______________ and ______________ .

6 Her hat did not have a ______________ in it.

7 The washroom on the plane had a ________________ in it.

8 There was some ________________ in the washroom.

9 When Mrs. Grant was ________________ her face and hands and putting up her hair, the hat was ________________ .

10 Before ________________ and ________________ her hair, Mrs. Grant took the hairpins out of it.

11 After brushing and combing her hair, she put the ________________ back in.

12 She put her ________________ and ________________ back in her bag and then took her ________________ out of another bag.

The Grants were in Chicago from Wednesday to Saturday. On Friday Mr. Grant went to the bus station and got three tickets to Salt Lake City. He went to the ticket office and said, "How much are three tickets to Salt Lake City? One is for my son, who is seven."

The man said, "Your son's ticket is $37.40. The other tickets are $74.80."

Mr. Grant gave two hundred dollars to the man, and the man gave $13.00 and three tickets to him.

"Is there a bus to Salt Lake City in the morning?"

"Yes," said the man. "One goes at 5:30 and another at 10:15."

"We will take the 10:15 bus," said Mr. Grant.

"Be here a little before that time," said the man.

"Yes, we will," said Mr. Grant. "Thank you."

On Saturday the Grants took a taxi to the bus station. They got on the bus at 10:05. Peter got a seat by the window. His mother was at his side and his father had a seat in front of them.

Pages **2-15**

That day their bus went through a part of two states, Illinois and Iowa. When they got to Des Moines, Iowa, the street lights were on. They went into the bus station for some food. Then they went back to the bus.

By this time Peter was ready for bed. His father put down the back of his seat for him. Now the seat was like a bed. His mother put something soft under his head and a coat over him. That is how Peter went to bed on the bus.

The Grants were on the bus a part of Saturday and all of Sunday. When they got to Salt Lake City, their friends, Mr. and Mrs. William Price, were at the bus station waiting for them. After shaking hands, Mr. Price said to Mr. Grant, "Please let me have your bags." Mr. Grant let him take one bag. Then the Prices took the Grants back to their house with them.

<u>Sunday</u> <u>Friday</u> <u>taxi</u>

<u>Wednesday</u> <u>tickets</u> <u>like</u> <u>office</u>

<u>station</u> <u>two hundred dollars</u>

1 The Grants were in Chicago from ____________ to Saturday.

2 Mr. Grant got the bus tickets on ______________ .

3 The three ________________ together were $187.00.

4 Mr. Grant gave ________________ to the man in the ticket ________________ .

5 The Grants took a ________________ to the bus ________________.

6 The Grants were on the bus all of ________________ .

7 After Peter's father put down the seat on the bus, the seat was ________________ a bed.

Pages **2-15**

1. A hairpin is a pin ______________ for the hair.
2. A birdhouse is a ______________ for birds.
3. An eggbox is a ______________ for eggs.
4. A tablecloth is a ______________ for a table.
5. A toothbrush is a ______________ for the teeth.
6. A keyhole is a ______________ for a key.
7. A hatpin is a ______________ for a hat.
8. A flowerpot is a ______________ for flowers.
9. A hairbrush is a ______________ for the hair.
10. A breadbox is a ______________ for bread.

Pages **2-15**

days rails week cents bells engine

Monday Saturday little much

Thursday Tuesday railroad Wednesday

1 Some clocks have ________________ which give the time.

2 A ________________ is seven ________________ .

3 A ________________ is a road of ________________.

4 To a person ten cents is very ________________ money.

5 There are a hundred ________________ in a dollar.

6 One dollar isn't ________________ money to some persons.

7 The ________________ is the part of a train which makes it go.

8 ________________ comes after Sunday and before ________________ .

9 ________________ comes after Tuesday and before ________________ .

10 ________________ comes between Friday and Sunday.

washing combing boiling

waiting brushing

1 You are ________________ your hair when you are putting a comb through it.

2 You are ________________ your coat when you go over it with a brush.

3 You get a thing clean by ________________ it with soap and water.

4 When water is ________________, it gives off steam.

5 ________________ for a train in a cold station makes a person cold.

Pages **2-15**

<u>Shaking</u> <u>Please</u> <u>how</u> <u>friends</u> <u>Let</u>

1 ________________ hands with a person is like saying, "We are friends."

2 When a person is shaking his hand like this, he is not saying, "We are ________________ ."

3 What we are and ________________ much we have are two different things.

4 Persons will do things for you when you say, "________________."

5 When a man sees a woman with a number of bags, he says, "________________ me take your bags for you."

Pages **2-15**

1 A door which is not shut is ___open___ .

2 Trousers which are not clean are ______________ .

3 Hands which are not dry are ______________ .

4 Cloth which is not thick is ______________ .

5 A building which is not high is ______________ .

6 Fruit which is not good is ______________ .

7 A dress which is not new is ______________ .

8 Hair which is not short is ______________ .

9 Milk which is not cold is ______________ .

10 Our eyes are not in the back of our heads but in the ______________ .

Pages **14-24**

Put the right words in the boxes.

Yesterday	Today	Tomorrow
Saturday	**Sunday**	Monday
Monday		
		Saturday
	Monday	

Monday			
Tuesday			
Wednesday	**Yesterday**	**today**	**tomorrow**
Thursday	today		
Friday	tomorrow		

This is a room in a school______ (education, school).

The teacher is at the ______________ (board, paper). He

is ______________ (learning, teaching) English. The men

and women are ______________ (learning, teaching)

English. They went to ______________ (education, school)

when they were boys and girls, but English was not part

of their______________ (education, school). Now they

are ______________ (getting, living) in the United States.

Pages **16-25**

The ______________ (board, teacher) is writing letters on the ______________ (board, teacher). The men and women are ______________ (reading, writing) the letters on ______________ (paper, pens) with their ______________ (paper, pens). They will put some of the ______________ (letters, words) together and make ______________ (letters, words). They do not have much English, but in time reading and writing English will not be hard for them.

This man is writing a letter. He is writing to the editor of the newspaper which he gets. An editor is one of the men who do work for the newspaper. He says what will get into the newspaper. This is what Mr. Penn is writing:

1320 South Street
Littleton, Ohio
May 16, 2004

The Town Times
45 High Street
Littleton, Ohio

Dear Sir:

I saw the story in your newspaper on what Senator Fillimaster said in Washington. Your paper said that Senator Fillimaster is not right, but I say that he is right.

Senator Fillimaster said that there was money in Washington for education. He said, "Let Washington give this money to the states and then the states will give it to the towns. When this money goes to the towns of the United States, all of them will have money for good buildings and good teachers."

Cities are very great towns. They have money for good school buildings and good teachers. But towns like this one in which we are living do not have much money for education. There are a great number of boys and girls, and the old school buildings will not take them all. Towns like this one put all their money into new school buildings, and there isn't money for the teachers, who do very hard work. How will we get good teachers when we give them little money?

Your newspaper said, "Education is not the work of the men in Washington. When the men in Washington give money to us, the education of our boys and girls will be in their hands. Let Washington keep its money. Education is the work of the towns."

Like Senator Fillimaster, I say that this is a question of money, and Washington has the answer. Washington will not keep us from doing the right things with this money. But with little money we will not have good schools or good teachers, and then how will we have good education?

Yours truly,

Percival Penn

Percival Penn

Pages **16-25**

1 Mr. Penn was living in a ______________ (town, city).

2 Senator Fillimaster said that when Washington gives money to the ________________ (states, cities), then they will give it to the towns.

3 ________________ (Towns, Cities) have a great number of persons in them.

4 Ohio is a ________________ (state, city).

5 New York City is a ________________ (town, city).

There! Mr. Penn put his pen down and took up the letter. After reading it over four times, he said, "This is a very good letter. Now I will put it in the letter box."

He then put on his hat and coat. He went out of the house and down the front steps to the street. There was a letter box on the other side of the street. Before he put the letter into the letter box, he took a look at the front of it. "Oh!" he said. "There is no stamp on this!"

He went back into the house. He went through all the drawers in his writing table, but there were no stamps.

"Dorothy," he said, "do you have some stamps?"

Mrs. Penn was coming into the room with a postcard in her hand. "There isn't a stamp in the house," she said. "Are you going to the post office?"

Mr. Penn said, "I wasn't going, but now I will. Do you have a letter ready for the post?"

"This is a postcard to our friend, Susan. I put two or three lines on the back of it, saying, We will come and see you on Saturday. Percy sends his love."

"Good," said Mr. Penn. "I will take it with my letter to the post office and get some stamps."

"Get a hundred," said Mrs. Penn. "Then we will not be going to the post office every day."

Pages **16-25**

<u>friend</u> <u>house</u> <u>steps</u> <u>hundred</u> <u>sends</u>

<u>postcard</u> <u>out of</u> <u>post office</u>

<u>stamp</u> <u>love</u> <u>letter</u> <u>street</u>

1 After he put his hat and coat on, Mr. Penn went ________________ the house and down the front ________________ .

2 He went to the letter box on the other side of the ________________ .

3 He had his ________________ in his hand.

4 There was no ________________ on the letter.

5 He went back into the ________________ .

6 Mrs. Penn was writing a ________________ to their ________________ , Susan.

7 On the back of the card Mrs. Penn said, "Percy ________________ his ________________ ."

8 Mr. Penn will go to the ________________ and get a ________________ stamps.

On the back page of the newspaper which Mr. Penn got, there was a part for letters like the one which he sent. Two days went by before his letter got into the paper, but, then, there it was with three other letters. He took a good look at it. Yes, the words were the same ones which he put in the letter.

Two of the other three letters had questions in them. Under these letters there was a short answer from the editor.

One letter was on the same story of Senator Fillimaster. The man who sent this letter to the newspaper was a Mr. Gordon White. He and Mr. Penn were living on the same street, but not at the same number. They sent their letters to the newspaper on the same day, but they did not say the same thing. Here is Mr. White's letter:

> 1851 South Street Littleton, Ohio May 16, 2004 The Town Times 45 High Street Littleton, Ohio Dear Sir, The story in your newspaper on Senator Fillimaster was very good. You are right. Let Senator Fillimaster and his friends in Washington keep their hands off our schools. Yours truly, Gordon White

Pages **16-25**

Put Mr. White's letter on these lines:

in the post office | in an office
in a waiting room | in a school room
in a harbor | in a taxi

1 This man is ______________________

____

2 This man is ______________________

____

3 This man is ______________

______________________________.

4 This woman is ____________

______________________________.

5 This boy is ______________

______________________________.

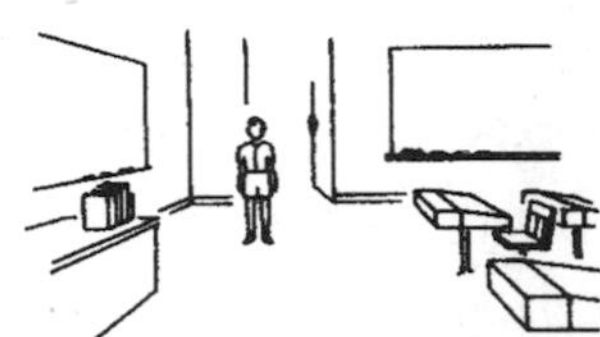

6 This ship is ______________

______________________________.

Philip Harrington is a newspaper man writing for a great city paper. His work takes him to different parts of the city and lets him see what is going on there. By questioning persons in the streets he gets together stories for the newspaper and takes or sends them to his office. Reading these stories is the work of another man on the paper. Philip does the work of a reporter and the other man is an editor. That is their work.

From the windows of the newspaper office, which is high up in a downtown building, one sees the water on a clear day. The city has a great harbor with ships coming in from everywhere. Philip's editor sent him to the harbor one day to get a story about the men out of work. Dock workers (men who put things on and take them off ships in the harbor) were getting $12.47 an hour at that time and were saying they were not happy. This was not very much for the hard work they did.

Philip went from one to another of the men on the streets near the harbor, questioning them and their friends and writing down what they said. "We will go

back to work when we get $13.80 an hour, but not before," said the men. Philip put this into his story for the paper, and he put other things into it–what other men said of these dock workers who kept ships in harbor and kept others from making journeys which they were ready and waiting to make. He gave a picture of the families of these men out of work. There were different sides to the question and Philip's story made them clear. When he saw it, the editor put Philip's story on the front page of the paper and that made Philip very happy.

Philip Harrington is one of two men who will be sent to Switzerland by their newspaper in a short time. He will be there for three weeks. Men and women from all parts of the earth will be in Switzerland together when the two men are there. Philip will send stories of what these men and women say and do to his editor in the United States. The other man will send pictures. Journeys like this are hard work. Philip will be doing a great part of his writing at night and sending his stories to his editor before morning. In a day or two men and women in the United States will be reading these stories and seeing the pictures of what is going on in Europe.

Pages **16-25**

Put the parts of one story under Picture A and the other under Picture B.

He is going to his work in the newspaper office.
This is Philip.
It is night in Switzerland.
When he gets to the office, he will see Philip's story.
This is the editor.
He is in his room writing a story.
It is morning.
He will send the story over to his editor before morning.

Picture A

1 It is night in Switzerland.

2 ____________________

Pages **16-25**

3 ____

____

4 ____

____

____

Picture B

1 ____

2 ____

3 ____

____

4 ____

____

____

<u>pictures</u>   <u>newspaper</u>   <u>front</u>

<u>great</u>   <u>pages</u>   <u>look</u>

1 This man has a ____________________ in his hands.

2 He is taking a ____________________ at it.

3 We see all of the ____________________ page.

4 We see parts of the other ________________ .

5 There are two ________________ on the front page.

6 There are a ________________ number of words on the front page.

Pages **16-25**

Put a line through anything which is not right.

1 Every tree has roots.

2 Every woman has long hair.

3 Every day the sun comes up.

4 Every day you say the same things.

5 Every week has seven days in it.

6 Every family has five persons in it.

7 Every cow is an animal.

8 Every animal is a cow.

Pages **16-25**

<u>sky</u> <u>cloud</u> <u>moon</u> <u>stars</u>

<u>sun</u> <u>night</u> <u>directions</u>

1 The heat from the ________________ keeps us warm, but when a ________________ is between us and the sun, we do not get much heat or light.

2 At night the ________________ gives a little light to us, but its light comes from the sun.

3 We do not see the sun at ________________ .

4 On a night when there are no clouds, we see a great number of ________________ in the sky.

5 North, South, East and West are four ______________ .

Pages **16-25**

In this picture, the word 'East' is on the line east of the earth. Put the right words on the other lines.

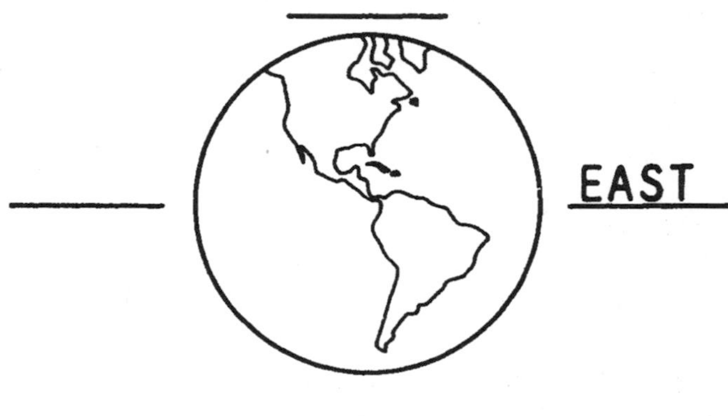

<u>sent</u> <u>sending</u> <u>send</u>

1 Mrs. Johnson will ______ the box to her son James after putting his name on it, the name of his street and town, and the right number of stamps.

2 Now she is in the post office. She is ________ the box to James.

3 James was happy when he got the box which his mother ___________ . It had food in it.

Pages **22-24**

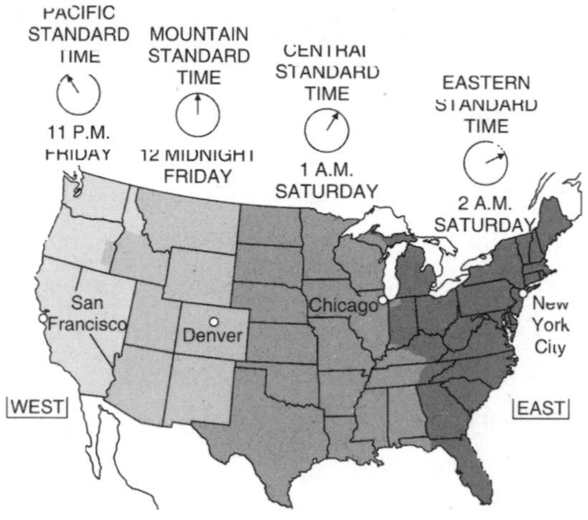

The earth goes round from east to west. Cities in the East of the United States get the light of the sun before cities in the West. It is 6 a.m. or six in the morning in New York City before it is 6 a.m. in Chicago, and it is 6 a.m. in Chicago before it is 6 a.m. in San Francisco.

Let us say that now it is 8 a.m. on Tuesday in New York City. Then it is 7 a.m. in Chicago, 6 a.m. in Denver, and 5 a.m. in San Francisco. The men and women in New York City are going to work, but those in San Francisco will be in bed for another hour or two. The time of day in the two cities is different, but it is the same day.

There are times when it is not the same day in the two cities. When it is 10 p.m. (ten at night) in San Francisco, it is 11 p.m. on the same day in Denver, 12 at night or 12 midnight, as we say, in Chicago, and 1 a.m. in the morning on Wednesday in New York City. It is Wednesday in New York City before it is Wednesday in San Francisco.

When a man goes from New York City to Chicago, he will "make" time by putting the hands of the clock back one hour. The day of his journey will be twenty-five hours long. When a person goes from New York City to San Francisco the day of his journey will be twenty-seven hours long. But the day he comes back east will be twenty-one hours.

Some planes go from New York City to San Francisco in three hours. A person who gets on one of these planes in New York City at 4 p.m. New York time will get off the plane in San Francisco at 4 p.m. San Francisco time! That day will be twenty-seven hours long for him, but it will be twenty-four hours long for us.

Pages **22-25**

<u>round</u> <u>before</u> <u>p.m.</u> <u>hours</u> <u>east</u> <u>night</u>

<u>west</u> <u>a.m.</u> <u>after</u> <u>morning</u> <u>hour</u>

1 The earth goes ____________ from east to west.

2 Cities in the ____________ of the United States get the light of the sun after cities in the____________ .

3 When it is 9 in the morning, we say it is 9____________ and when it is 9 at night, we say it is 9____________ .

4 It is 2 a.m. in San Francisco ____________ it is 2 a.m. in New York City.

5 It is 11 p.m. in Denver____________ it is 11 p.m. in San Francisco.

6 When a person goes from Denver to New York City, the clocks are two____________ different when he gets there.

7 When a person goes from New York City to Chicago, the clocks are one ____________ different when he gets there.

8 When it is 2 on Saturday____________ in New York City, it is 11 on Friday ____________ in San Francisco.

These two men are in front of the lockers in a bus station. The man on the left has his things in locker number 3713. He will take them out. He has the key of the locker in his hand. The man on the right will put his bag in locker number 3718. Which lockers have things in them and which do not?

The lockers which have things in them are:

3713 three thousand seven hundred thirteen

The lockers which do not have things in them are:

This is a street. The man who is going down the left side of the street is in front of house number 1614. He will go by the other houses on the left which have these numbers: 1616, 1618, 1620 and 1622. Another man is on the right side of the street. He is at the door of his house. His house is number 1615. What are the numbers of the other houses on this side of the street? The numbers are:

1615 one thousand six hundred fifteen

Pages **30-39**

<u>attempt</u> <u>something</u> <u>enough</u>

<u>bent</u> <u>straight</u> <u>better</u>

Will William get up into the tree?

1 No, his arms are not long ____________. But now his brother Jack is with him.

2 With his brother there, William is making another ____________. Jack's back is____________.

3 Now his back is ____________again and William is up in the tree.

4 This attempt was ____________.

Jack goes off. Will William go up high in the tree?

No, there are not enough branches for getting up high. But William is happy where he is. He takes a look round him.

5 William sees______________________down on the grass, but he does not see what it is. Is it some sort of animal?

No, it is his brother Jack down on his hands and knees. He is saying, "Where is my knife? It was in my pocket."

1 This bird has a
__________________ of
food in its mouth.

2 Their mouths are open
___________________.

3 This is a cloth bag. It has food for animals in it. A man will get the bag open with the ________________ of his knife.

4 He is making a
_________________ in the
cloth with the knife.

Pages **31-38**

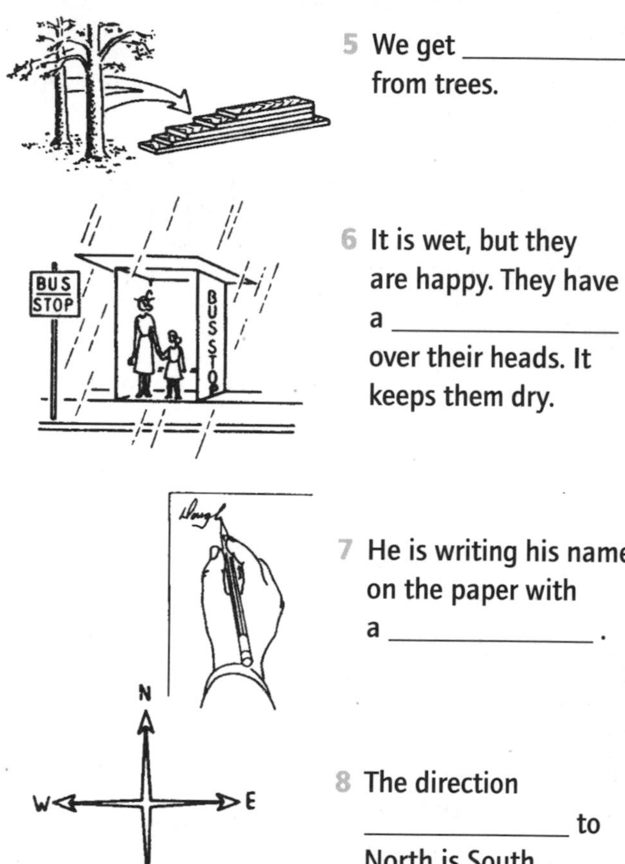

5 We get ______________
from trees.

6 It is wet, but they
are happy. They have
a ________________
over their heads. It
keeps them dry.

7 He is writing his name
on the paper with
a _______________ .

8 The direction
_______________ to
North is South.

Pages **34-43**

nails down support middle

up hammer end

This is a see-saw. Mr. Carter will make one for his sons, Barry and Ben. He will make a strong support and then he will put a long, smooth board over it.

Here is Mr. Carter. He is making the ______________ for the see-saw. He has a ______________ in his hands. He is putting the parts of the support together with ______________ . When the support is ready, he will put a board over it. The support will be under the ______________ of the board.

Barry and Ben are on the see-saw. Barry is at one ______________ and Ben is at the other. Barry is up and Ben is ______________ . When Barry comes down, Ben will go ______________ .

Pages **34-43**

<u>together</u> <u>broken</u> <u>strong</u> <u>better</u>

<u>bent</u> <u>stronger</u> <u>enough</u> <u>straight</u>

Now another boy is on the see-saw with Barry and Ben. He is at one end and Barry and Ben are ____________ at the other. The board is ____________ . When there were two boys on it, it was ____________ .

Now the board is ____________ . It was enough ________________ for two boys but not strong ______________ for three. Mr. Carter will get a ______________ board. Then Barry and Ben will have a ______________ see-saw.

<u>cutting</u>   <u>wider</u>   <u>angle</u>   <u>right</u>

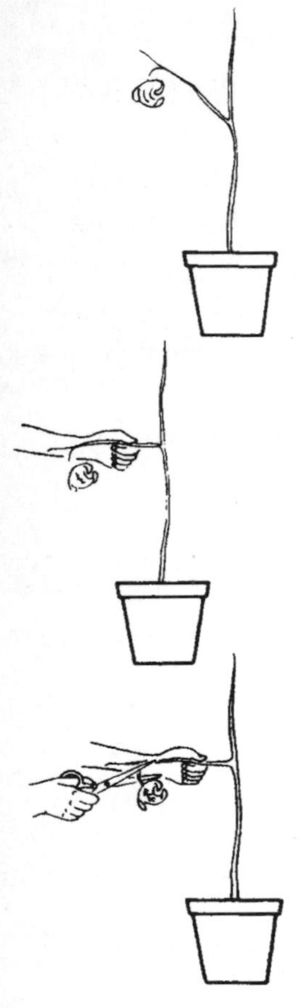

1 The branch of this plant and its stem come together at an ____________.

2 The woman is taking the branch in her hand. Now the angle is ____________ than it was before.

3 Now it is a ____________ angle.

4 The woman is ____________ the leaf off the branch.

Page **42**

The answer which the book gives is short. Make your answer a shorter one.

1 Question: When will the food be ready?
Answer: It is ready now.
Your answer: It's ready now.

2 Question: Do you keep the dog in the house all day?
Answer: No, I do not.
Your answer: ______________________

3 Question: Were you in New York City this weekend?
Answer: No, I was not.
Your answer: ______________________

4 Question: What is the time?
Answer: It is four.
Your answer: ______________________

5 Question: Is that your hat?
Answer: No, it is not.
Your answer: ______________________

6 Question: What are you doing with those bags in your hands?
Answer: I am going south for a week.
Your answer: ______________________

Paul went into the room where his mother was making a dress on a sewing machine.

This is a sewing machine. Paul saw the machine.

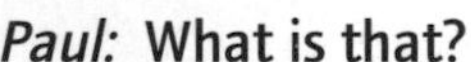

Paul: What is that?

Mother: This is the new sewing machine which your father got for me. It is an instrument for making clothing.

Paul: What are you______________(do, doing) with it?

Mother: I am making a dress.

Paul: Oh, the_____________ (collar, coat) of your dress goes up, not down! And there are the______________(buttonholes, buttons). But they are not open!

Mother: No, they are not. I made them by machine. I made the buttonholes in your coat by hand, but that takes a longer time. Now, see, I am making

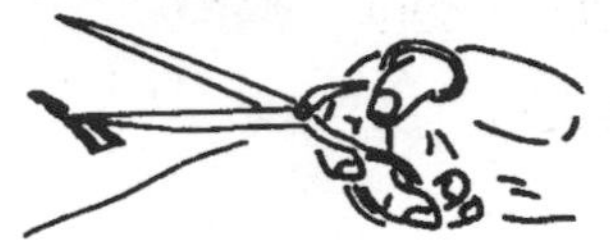

a_______________ (narrow, wide) cut down the middle of this one with the _______________ (dress, scissors). There! It is open now.

Paul: Are these buttons going on the dress?

Mother: Yes, some machines put them on, but my machine does not. I will put them on by hand.

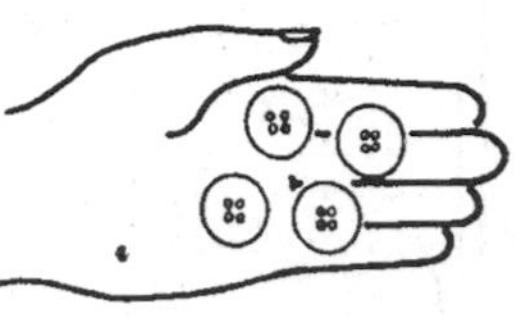

Paul: Here they are.

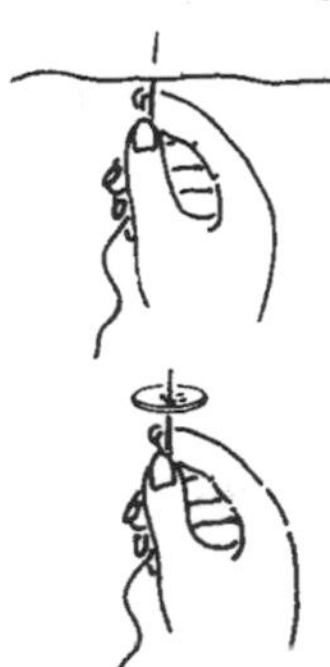

Mother: Give one of them to me and put the others on the table. I am putting the _______________(knife, needle) and _______________(cord, thread) through the cloth of the dress. Now the needle is going through a hole in the________ (blade, button). I put a zipper in the side of my dress with the machine. Here is a picture of a zipper. Do you see all the little teeth?

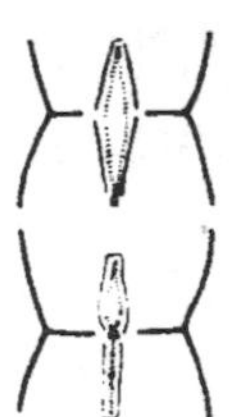

Paul: Yes, they come together when the zipper is shut.

Pages **55-57**

spring months because April March

quarter May stronger flowers

This is a calendar. It is a picture calendar. It has twelve pictures in it ______________ there are twelve ______________ in a year.

This is a picture of spring. There are ______________ at the side of the road. The spring months are ______________, ______________, and ______________. In ______________ the days get longer and the heat of the sun gets ______________. The three spring months make a ______________ of the year.

<u>sun</u> <u>half</u> <u>than</u> <u>June</u> <u>warm</u>

<u>July</u> <u>summer</u> <u>August</u>

This is a picture of summer. Men, women, boys and girls are out in the ________________. The summer months are ________________ , ________________ , and ________________. In ________________the days are longer________________ the nights. The air is ________________. The spring and summer months together make one ________________of a year.

quarters November shorter falling

fall October September

This is a picture of fall. The leaves are ______________ off the trees. The fall months are ________________ , ________________ , and ________________ .

The days are getting ________________ . Spring, summer and ________________ together make three ________________ of a year.

<u>December</u> <u>winter</u> <u>year</u> <u>January</u>

<u>snow</u> <u>February</u> <u>nights</u>

This is a picture of winter. There is________________ over everything. The winter months are ________________ , ________________, and ________________ . In ________________ the days are shorter than the ________________ . The spring, summer, fall, and winter months together make one ____________________ .

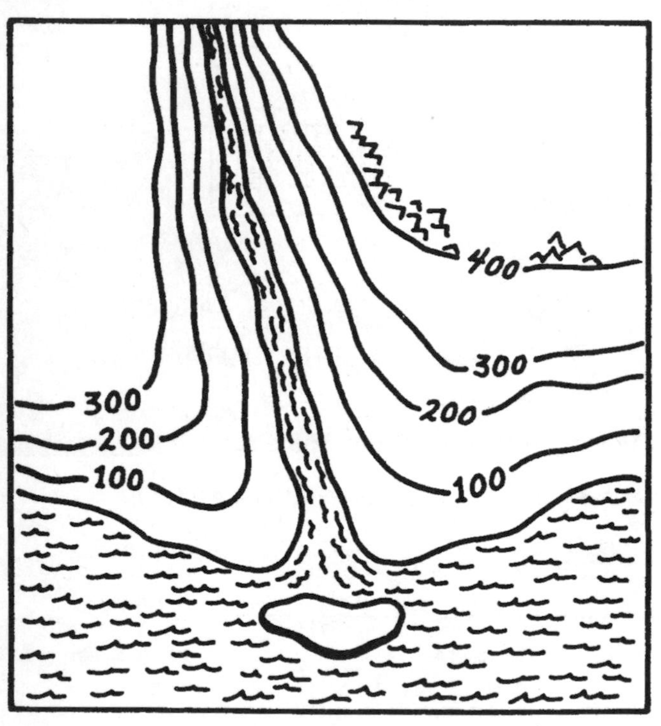
400
300
200
100
300
200
100

Pages **55-71**

<u>government</u> <u>land</u> <u>instruments</u> <u>island</u> <u>map</u>

<u>sea</u> <u>near</u> <u>distances</u> <u>river</u> <u>pictures</u>

On the opposite page is a ________________ . The lines with the numbers on them say how high the ________________ is. Near the ______________it goes up to 400 feet. ________________ the ______________ it is not more than 100 feet. All the land on the ________________ is under 100 feet.

The________________ makes maps like this. Men and women go up in airplanes and take _______ of the land. Others go over the land on foot, taking ______________ with them for measuring ______________ and getting directions.

Pages **57-69**

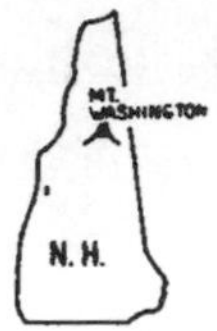

Mount Washington is a mountain in the state of New Hampshire. It is 6,288 _______________ (feet, miles) high. A person _______________(map, may) go up this mountain by automobile, by train or on foot.

The Carriage Road is for _______________ (automobiles, planes). It is eight _______________ (miles, yards) long. Going up the mountain by automobile takes _______________ (about, more) half an hour. Going up by train takes one hour and forty-five _______________ (inches, minutes), and coming down takes forty-five minutes. The journey down is _______________ (quick, quicker) than the journey up, but _______________ (slow, slower) than the journey by automobile.

Walking up Mt. Washington is a _______________ (soft, slow) journey. The _______________ (distance, measure) on foot may or may not be greater than by automobile or train, but going on foot takes _______________ (equal, more) time. There are numbers of trails; trails are roads for those who are walking.

Going up Mt. Washington is ________________ (equal, sometimes) like going from summer into winter. A ________________ (dark, quick) change in the direction of the wind may make a warm, bright day into a cold, dark one. Sometimes clouds will come down in a minute or two and put a ______________ (clear, thick) cover over everything. A person may see no more than two ________________(miles, yards) in front of him. When he gets into the thickest cloud, he may see no more than a number of ________________ (inches, distance).

Walking in the mountains is for persons who have warm clothing, strong shoes, food and a ______________ (map, river) with them. One who does not take these things may have a bad time. Some take a ____________ (stick, yard) with them.

A ____________ (walk, walking) on a mountain and a walk in a city may be ______________ (equal, same) in distance, but they are not the same thing at all. Walking in the mountains is hard work, but those with a love for mountains are happy doing it.

Pages **59-62**

The Wilsons are a family of five. Mr. and Mrs. Wilson have three boys: Arthur, James, and Joseph. Joseph came after the other two boys and James came after Arthur.

older   younger   oldest   youngest

A. 1 Arthur is the ___________.

2 James is ___________ than Joseph.

3 Joseph is the ___________.

4 He is ___________ than James and Arthur.

Here are three shirts.

cleaner   cleanest   dirtier   dirtiest

B. 1 The shirt on the left is the ___________.

2 It is ___________ than the other two.

3 The shirt in the middle is the ___________.

4 It is ___________ than the other two.

1 Here are three doors. The one on the right is the _____________ (thicker, thickest). It is _____________ (thicker, thickest) than the other two. The other two are not _____________ (as, than) thick _____________ (as, than) it is.

2 Here are three balls. The ball in the middle is _____________ (harder, hardest) than the one on the left, but not _____________ (as, than) hard _____________ (as, than) the one on the right. The one on the right is the _____________ (harder, hardest). The one on the left is the _____________ (softer, softest).

Pages **61-66**

1 The Nile River is 4,160 miles long. The Amazon River is 3,900 miles long, and the Ganges River is 1,540 miles long. The Nile is the ______________ (longer, longest) of the three. The Amazon is ______________ (longer, longest) than the Ganges.

2 Victoria Falls are four waterfalls together in the south of Africa. One of them, Leaping Waterfall, is 36 yards wide. Another, Main Fall, has two parts 573 and 525 yards wide, and another, Rainbow Fall is 600 yards wide. Leaping Waterfall is the ______________(widest, narrowest) of these falls and Rainbow Fall is the ______________(widest, narrowest).

Changes in transport are going on all the time. Before 1800, men and women made journeys on foot, horseback, ship, and by carriage, much as others before them did. Through the years, they made better ships and carriages, but the changes were not very great.

Great changes in transport came after 1800. First there was the steam engine of James Watt, and then came the steam carriage, the steamship, and the train. After Robert Fulton's steamship, the *Clermont*, there were more and more steamships on rivers, and before long, steamships were going over the sea between America and Europe.

Between 1820 and 1830, there were numbers of steam carriages on the roads of England. These were like horse carriages with no horses. A steam engine made them go. In 1814 George Stephenson made an engine for a train of carriages, four or five or six in line, and in a short time, trains were taking the place of horses and steam carriages.

Men were making automobiles in Europe and the United States before 1900. By 1913, Henry Ford was putting automobiles onto the roads of the United States in great numbers. Before that, roads were opening through the sky. The Wright brothers gave us a new sort of transport in 1903 when they went up in their first airplane. Airplanes are the quickest sort of transport. Today they go through the air at six hundred miles an hour or more.

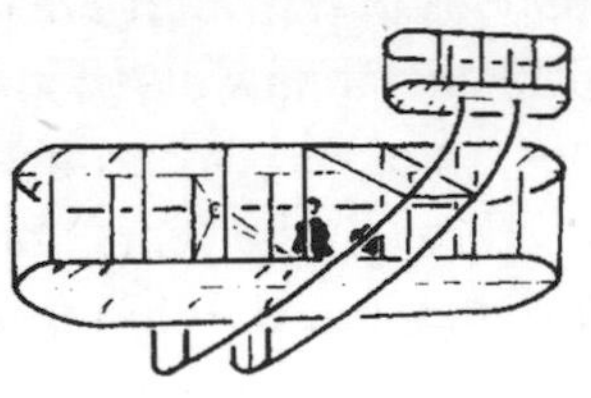

Now greater changes are taking place than ever before. We are making new sorts of transport – transport which takes off from our earth for greater and greater distances. By the year 2050, great numbers of us may be making journeys to the moon and other places far from the earth.

You will give answers to these questions:

1 What changes in transport came between 1800 and 1900?

The changes in transport which came between 1800 and 1900 were the steam carriage, the steamship, and the train.

2 By the year 2050, what new journeys may your sons and daughters be making?

3 What sorts of transport are there for journeys on land? over the water? through the air?

"Our street is _____________ (equal, changing). It is getting more and more buildings on it. It is getting _____________ (ever, full) of buildings," said David Martin. "The day will come when the tall buildings round us will keep the sunlight from coming in the windows and it will be _____________ (bright, dark) all day long in here."

Mary Martin went over to the window by David and took a look at the new building going up on the other side of the street.

"Let's get a place with three or four rooms in a building which is very high. Then we'll have sunlight some part of the day," she said.

"High up in the building there is more light and air and the rooms are _____________ (brighter, darker)."

"But the _____________ (price, why) of places like that is as high as the building it is in and we do not have enough money for it. Let's go somewhere where there is some _____________ (land, more) round a little house. Then we will get enough sunlight and we will not see buildings in every direction."

"Yes, ______________ (sometimes, why) don't we?" said Mary.

They got into their automobile and went to the office of a friend, who said to them, "I have the right house for you. Come and see it."

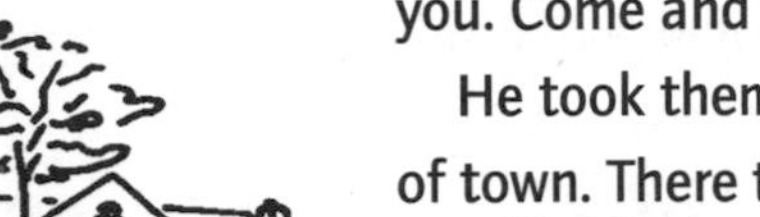

He took them four miles out of town. There they saw a new little house with some land round it. There were trees between the house and the other houses.

"Did you______________ (about, ever) see a better house?" said David to Mary.

"No, I never did," said Mary. "But how much is it?"

The price didn't make David very happy. But the man said to him, "By putting a little money down for the house now, you may go right into it. It will be your house. After that, the money which you put out every month will be no more than what you are giving for the place where you are living now."

"Good," said David. "That is what we will do."

Pages **30-71**

1 Some places in the U.S. are far ____________ (from, to) one another.

2 The distance from one place ____________ (to, of) another may be great.

3 A person may do different things ____________ (with, for) his money.

4 It is bad when a train goes ____________ (off, on) its rails.

5 When we see the earth ____________(from, of) the north, we see more land than water.

6 Flowers keep their faces ____________ (to, at) the sun.

7 Making buttonholes ____________(for, on) buttons is work.

8 A plane may go a great distance ____________ (in, of) an hour.

9 When you go out of your house, keep some money with you ____________ (at, to) all times.

10 There are three feet ____________ (in, on) a yard.

1 Which girl has the long hair?

the girl on the

right.

2 Which man is saying, "Let me see the map?"

3 Which man is on an island?

4 Which are the government buildings?

1. Over the water is a springboard. The ____________ (spring, size) of the board makes it go down at the end where the boy is.

2. That is a ____________ (ball, black) in the air between the two men.

3. Because of the ____________ (attraction, wind) between the ball and the earth, the ball will come down.

4. The boy is putting his full ____________ (weight, fire) on the springboard.

5. The girl is making something good over the ____________(fire, first).

<u>greater</u> <u>nearer</u> <u>nearest</u> <u>farthest</u>

1 The water is ________________ to the house than the mountains.

2 The trees are the ______________ of all to the house.

3 The mountains are the __________________ of all from the house.

4 The distance from the mountains to the house is ________________ than the distance from the trees to the house.

Here are three women. They are of different ______________(sizes, springs). The one with the dog is ______________ (small, smaller) than the one with the ______________ (cord, stick). But she is not as ________________ (small, smaller) as the woman with the book. From left to right, the woman with the books is ________________ (first, last); the woman with the dog is in the ________________ (middle, end) and the woman with the stick is ________________ (first, last).

<u>statement</u>   <u>writer</u>   <u>meter</u>   <u>watch</u>

1 Writing is the work of a person who is a ____________________.

2 A __________________ is a measure of distance which is a little longer than a yard.

3 A __________________ is a very small clock which one may put in one's pocket or on one's wrist (lower arm).

4 "All men are equal" is a __________________ .

mind colder hanging square blows motion

1 This man is getting the right answer. He is writing the numbers with a pen, but he is doing a great part of the work with his mind.

2 This man is ________________ by his hands.

3 One picture is in a round frame. The other picture is in a ________________one.

Pages **81-89**

4 This man gave his coat to the woman because she was cold. Now he is _______________ than he was before, but he keeps saying that he is not cold.

5 He did not get on the bus because the bus was in

_______________ .

6 This rock is broken because the man gave it a number of _______________ with his hammer.

<u>one twenty-fifth</u> <u>science</u>

<u>pull</u> <u>idea</u> <u>if</u>

1 Men and women of _______________ are learning new things about the earth every day.

2 When a person makes a picture of a ship, he has an _________________ in his mind of what a ship is like.

3 There are twenty-five fours in one hundred. Four is _________________of a hundred.

4 Wind takes seeds from plants up into the air. When there is no more wind, the _______________ of the earth makes the seeds come down again.

5 _______________ the number of persons on the earth keeps getting greater and greater, some day there will not be enough room for all.

<u>cause</u> <u>motion</u> <u>rest</u> <u>effect</u> <u>true</u> <u>false</u>

1 The apples coming down off the branch are in _______________.

2 The apples round the boy's feet are at _______________.

3 The _______________ of the branch's motion is the boy's shaking it.

4 The _______________ of the boy's shaking the branch is its motion.

5 This is a_______________ statement about the picture: There are more apples round the boy's feet than on the branches.

6 This is a _______________ statement about the picture: The shaking made the apples come off.

Pages **81-89**

1 Inches and feet are measures of distance. What is a measure of weight?

____

____

2 What part of four pounds is one pound?

____

____

3 Here is a statement in numbers: "3 x 4 = 12." What is this statement in words?

____

____

4 What is an instrument for measuring weight?

____

____

5 What is the measure of distance which light goes in one year?

____

____

Pages **93-98**

Every day we get weather news. This news comes to us from weather stations. A weather station is a place where there are different weather instruments. Here are some of these instruments:

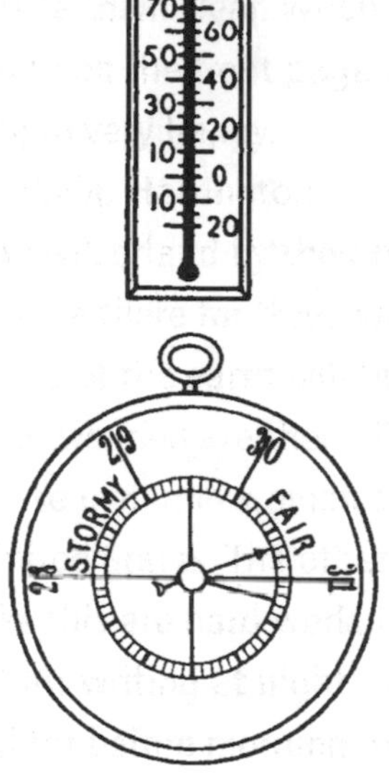

1 This is an instrument for measuring heat. It says how warm or cold the air is. When the air is cold, the liquid in the instrument comes down. When the air is warm, it goes up.

2 This is an instrument for measuring the weight of the air. Galileo was the first person who made the discovery that air has weight. Warm air goes up because it has less weight than cold air.

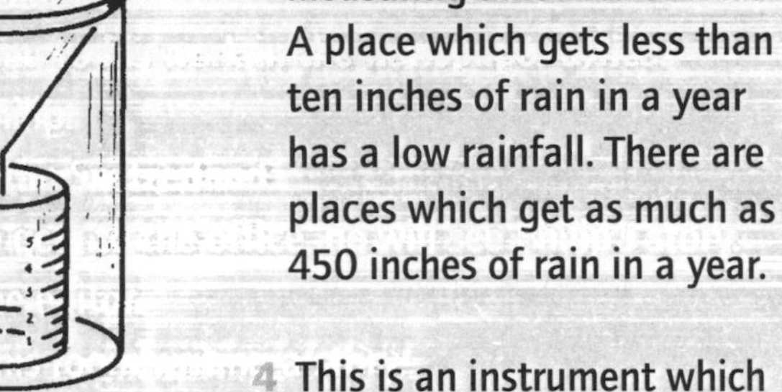

3 This is an instrument for measuring amounts of rain. A place which gets less than ten inches of rain in a year has a low rainfall. There are places which get as much as 450 inches of rain in a year.

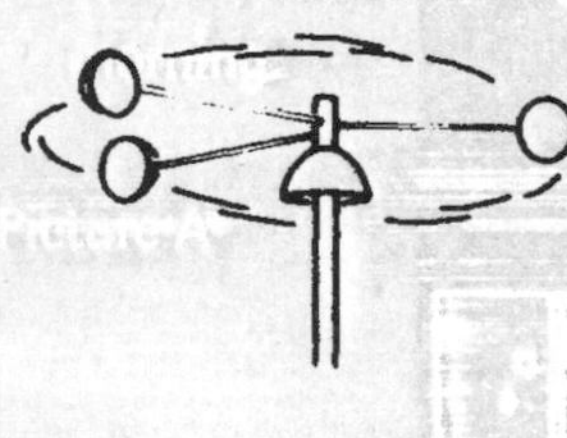

4 This is an instrument which says how strong the wind is. When the wind is blowing at ten miles an hour, it is not a strong wind. A wind of fifty miles an hour is a very strong wind. There are times when the wind goes more than a hundred miles an hour.

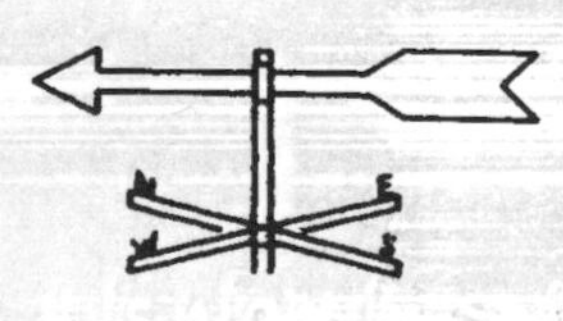

5 This is an instrument which gives the direction from which the wind is blowing. In the United States, the north wind is a cold wind and the south wind is a warm wind.

discovery only blowing less
drops weather worse amount

1 Galileo made the ______________ that air has weight.

2 Changes in the weather do not have one cause ______________.

3 A wind which is ______________ at fifty miles an hour is a very strong wind.

4 A place which gets ________________ than ten inches of rain in a year is very dry.

5 When it is raining, water comes down in __________ from the clouds.

6 When we get a number of wet, cold days, we say, "We are having bad ________________."

7 In the north of the United States the winters are ________________ than they are in the south.

8 The rainfall of a place is the ________________ of rain the place gets in a year.

1 When we see 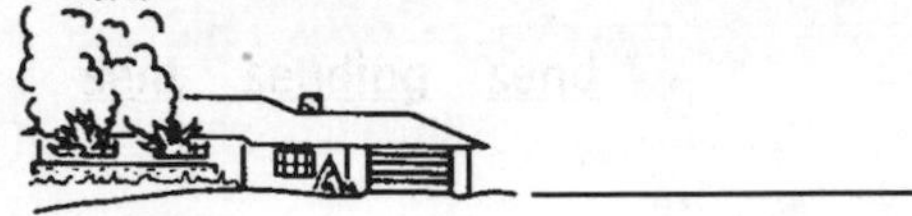 ______________

and fire coming out of a house, we say, "It is on fire." If the ______________ are very high and the ______________ is very thick, it is a bad fire.

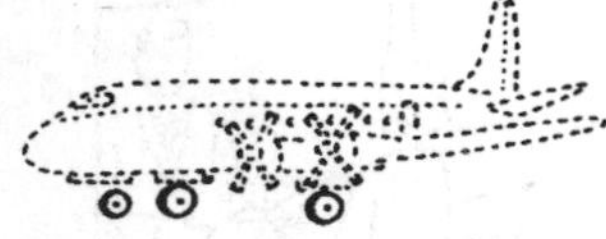

2 The ______________ of an airplane and the ______________ of a ship are different sorts of ______________ .

3 When a person with a great number of bags gets off a

train, a man with a

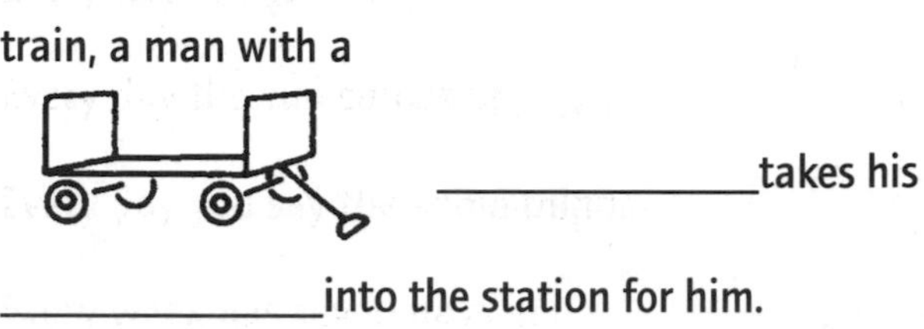

________________takes his

________________into the station for him.

4 In 1910 women had long

________________and in 1920 they

had ________________ ones.

5 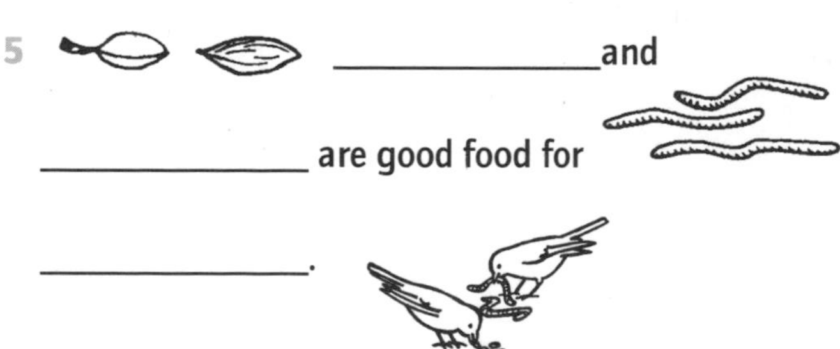

________________and

________________ are good food for

________________.

Page **99**

Make changes like the change in 1 for statements 2-6.

1 Why did he give his watch <u>to</u> you?

Why did he give you his watch?

2 I am very happy because he sent some flowers <u>to</u> me.

3 My father says that if I keep my room clean, he will give his old watch <u>to</u> me.

4 Don't get off the bus before giving some money <u>to</u> me.

5 He is writing a letter <u>to</u> Mother.

6 Did you give an answer <u>to</u> the girl?

Pages **80-89**

1 When science _______________ (puts, sends) a person on the moon, every newspaper has the story.

2 Getting ready for a journey to the moon _______________ (puts, takes) time.

3 The moon _______________(gets, makes) its light from the sun.

4 The sun _______________ (does, gives) light and heat to the earth.

5 Light _______________ (comes, puts) to the earth from the sun in about eight minutes.

6 The nearest star _______________ (makes, sends) its light to the earth, but its heat does not get to us.

7 A falling star_______________ (makes, does) a line of light across the sky.

8 The discovery of new stars _______________ (goes, takes) on all the time.

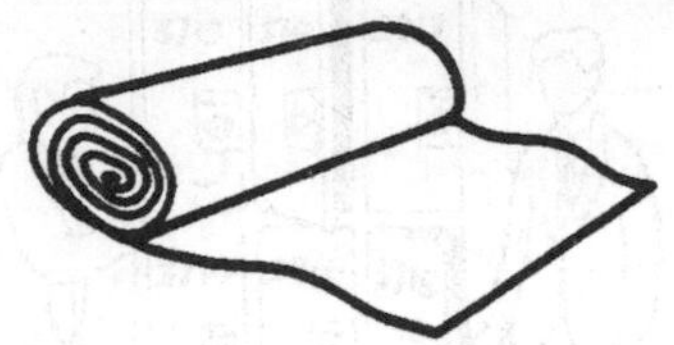

This is a_____________of cloth. There are different sorts of cloth. Cotton cloth comes from the __________ plant. It is of great use in making clothing for summer. Wool comes from ________________. It is soft and warm and makes good winter________________. Silk comes from ____________________. It makes a soft cloth which is ____________________ than cotton but not as warm as________________.

Pages **99-102**

In making cloth from wool,

Step one is cutting the wool off the sheep.

Step two is ______________________________.

Step three is ______________________________.

Step four is ______________________________.

Step five is ______________________________.

washing and drying the wool

putting the threads on a frame

making the threads into cloth

cutting the wool off the sheep

twisting the wool into threads

twists across silk warmer use

1. Mountain roads have a great number of ________________and turns in them.

2. Some roads go________________ the United States from east to west and are over 3000 miles long.

3. When it is winter in the north, the sea there is ________________ than the land.

4. A great amount of ________________ comes from China and Japan.

5. A cart with one wheel off is of no ________________.

Pages **103-107**

<u>rays</u> <u>herself</u> <u>point</u>

<u>seems</u> <u>seemed</u> <u>looking-glass</u>

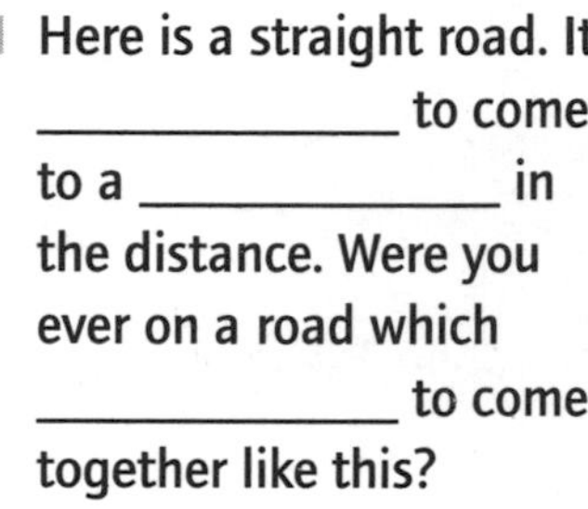

1 Here is a straight road. It ______________ to come to a ______________ in the distance. Were you ever on a road which ______________ to come together like this?

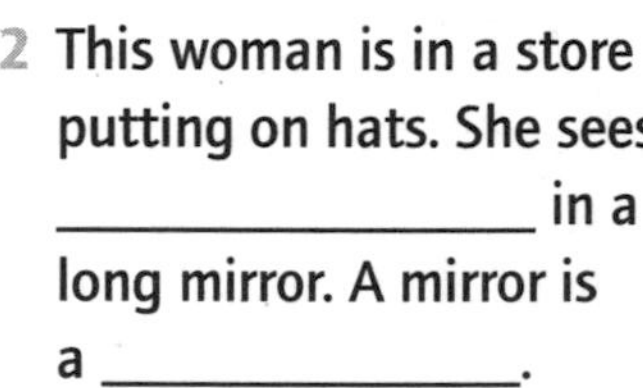

2 This woman is in a store putting on hats. She sees ________________ in a long mirror. A mirror is a ______________.

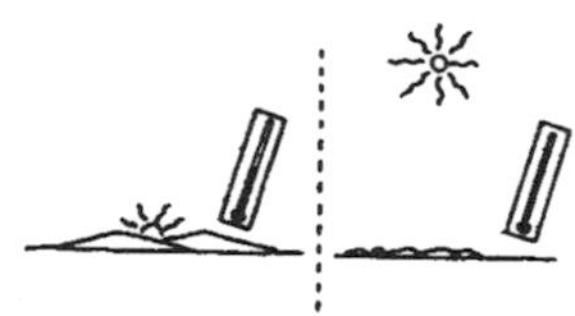

3 The sun's __________ give us more heat in the middle of the day than they do in the morning.

Pages **108-112**

Give questions for these answers. Put the right words on the lines in the answers.

1 Question: What does he have his foot on?

Answer: He has his foot on a spade.

2 Question: What ______________________________

______________________________?

Answer: She is ______________ with her needle.

Pages **108-112**

3 Question: Who ______________________________

____?

Answer: A __________________ makes use of a plow.

His work is __________________. His fields and

buildings are his __________________.

4 Question: Is ________________________________

____?

Answer: Yes, the man is __________________ his

________________ to get it ready for putting in seeds.

Pages **108-112**

5 Question: What ______________________________

____?

Answer: He makes _________________ and shoes for

a living. He is a ___________________.

6 Question: What ______________________________

____?

Answer: He has his __________________ in one

hand and his ________________ in the other. He is

a ________________.

Pages **108-112**

7 Question: What ______________________________

____?

Answer: Housekeeping is her work. She is

a ____________________.

8 Question: What sort __________________________

____?

Answer: He has a clothing store. He is a

____________________.

Pages **108-112**

9 Question: Where ______________________________

____?

Answer: This man goes to work in a bank every day. His work is ____________________.

10 Question: What ________________________________

____?

Answer: This businessman is keeping accounts for his _________________ .

Pages **109-110**

Gary Gill took a ________________ (direction, look) outside his door to see if he had a letter. He did. It was a statement from his ________________ (bank, bent), saying that he had $2,568.07 in his ________________ (account, amount).

"That money will not be there long," he said to himself. "There are ______________ (important, addition) things for me to do with it. Part of it will go for my schooling." He put the letter in his ______________ (pocket, middle) and put his coat on to go to a bookstore.

GARY GILL

BALANCE 2,568.07

At the bookstore he got three books with paper covers for his schoolwork. The ______________ (rest, prices) of the books were $9.50, $11.95, and $14.25. The storekeeper put the numbers down on some paper like this:

$ 9.50
11.95
14.25
36.30

Pages **109-110**

Gary saw the ______________ (numbers, needles) and said, "Is your ______________ (addition, question) right? I get a different answer."

The man did it again. "Your answer is right," he said. "it is 60 ______________ (cents, solids) less."

Then Gary said, "I don't have enough money with me. May I give you a ______________ (check, change)?"

"Yes, if you have something with your name on it," said the man.

"Here is something," said Gary, pulling out his bankbook and opening it. Then he took his checkbook and made out a check for the right amount.

Pages **111-123**

1 Talking to different sorts of men and women is part of Alfred's work _____________ (as, of) a newspaper man.

2 I got the name of your store _____________ (by, through) Ms. Stone.

3 Those pictures seem _____________ (to, with) me to be by the same painter.

4 How are you able to see _____________ (by, with) your hat over your eyes like that?

Pages **113-123**

Give short answers to these questions:

1 Which sort of drink does a person put sugar in, a sweet drink or a bitter one?

A bitter one

2 Which is more like bread – cake or butter?

3 Which is one of our five senses – touching or changing?

4 Which powder comes from mines in the earth – salt or sugar?

5 Which sense gives us knowledge of how soft or hard a thing is – smelling or touching?

6 Which part of your mouth is soft – your lips or your teeth?

Pages **113-123**

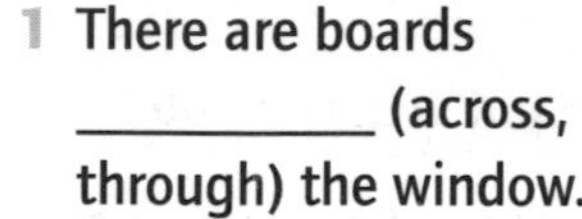

1 There are boards __________ (across, through) the window.

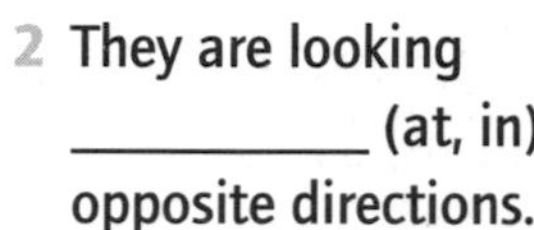

2 They are looking __________ (at, in) opposite directions.

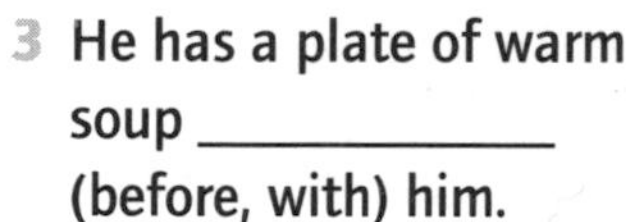

3 He has a plate of warm soup ___________ (before, with) him.

4 Mary's dress is very long. The woman will take it ___________ (up, off) with a needle and thread.

5 The roots of some plants have sugar ___________ (in, under) them.

Pages **114-122**

Put the right words on the right line.

1 We put sugar on food ______________________
____
____

2 A thing may seem strange __________________
____
____

3 We are able ____________________________
____
____

4 The two sides of a road seem ______________
____
____

5 An automobile is of great use ______________
____
____

to us when our house is far from our work.
to give it a sweet taste.
to come together in the distance.
to us if we have no knowledge of it.
to make mines which go deep down into the earth.

Put these words on the right line.

The grass	Her fingernails
The glasses	The sweet smell
The garden	The top

1 ______________ is up to his knees.

2 ______________ is full of flowers.

3 ______________ of the flowers is the cause of her smile.

4 ______________ are doing the work of scissors.

5 ______________ are on top of the books.

6 ______________ of this mountain has a cover of snow.

Pages **114-124**

<u>touch</u> <u>reading</u> <u>tasting</u> <u>hearing</u>

<u>smell</u> <u>seeing</u> <u>talking</u>

1 Through________________ food we are able to say if it is sweet or bitter or warm or cold.

2 Of the "five senses" ________________ gives us the greatest knowledge of our world.

3 The sense of ________________ may be more important to a dog than to a man.

4 Through ________________ books and newspapers we are able to get an idea of what is going on in the world.

5 It is chiefly our senses of seeing and of ____________ that give us knowledge of the size of something.

6 Through our senses of seeing and ________________ we get a knowledge of words and their uses.

7 Through writing and ________________ we are able to say what our ideas are.

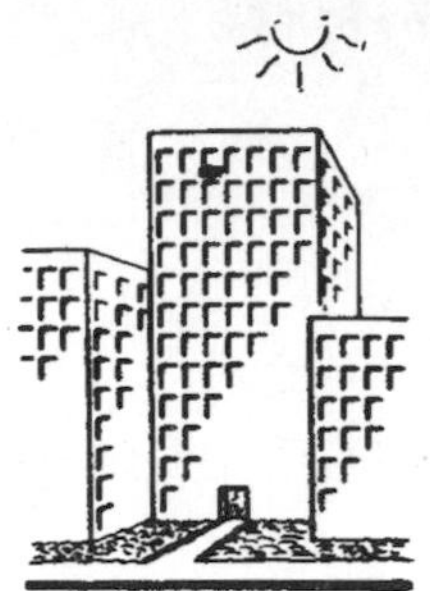

It is one of the first days of spring. The bright ________________ (red, yellow) sun is high in the sky. The sky is ______________ (blue, gray). Those men and women with rooms on this side of the building get the morning sun through their windows. But very little sunlight comes to the lower parts of the building. Here it is dark most of the day, and there is a little bit of snow. When it first came down it was ______________ (white, black), but now it is a dirty ______________ (gray, red) from the smoke of the buildings nearby.

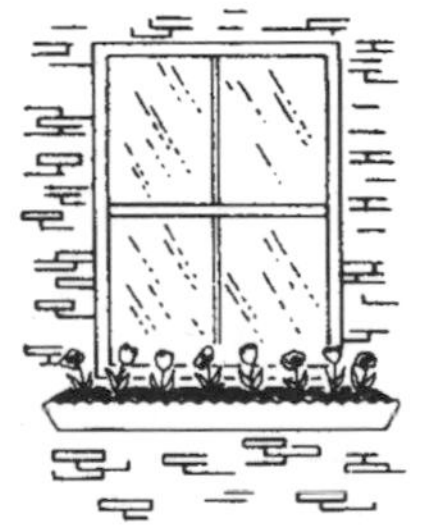

Under one of the windows is a flowerbox which gets enough sun for flowers to come up. The woman who has this room put some spring flower seeds in the window box one day, and now the young plants are coming up out of the earth. The flowers are different ___________ (collars, colors), but their leaves are all ____________ (green, blue). Some of the flowers are yellow and some ____________ (red, green) like the color of the woman's lips.

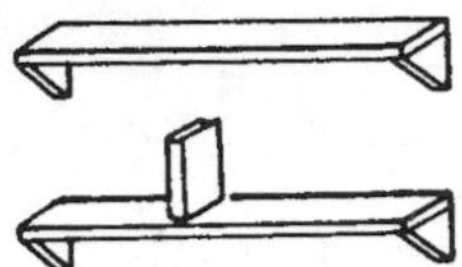

1 Is the book on the higher shelf?

No, it isn't.

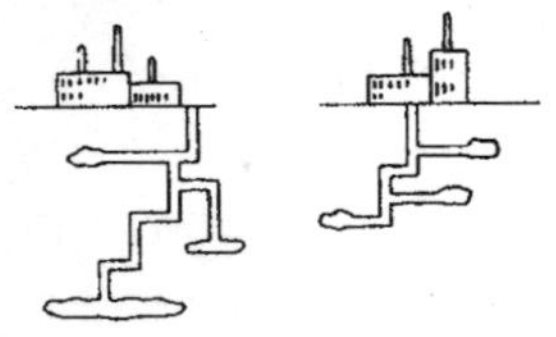

2 Is the mine on the left the deeper?

____

3 Is the boy on one of the lower branches?

____

4 Is the girl in the middle taller than the other two?

____

5 Is the man on the right thinner than the one on the left?

____

6 Does the girl have shorter hair than the boy?

____

<u>deeper</u> <u>longer</u> <u>taller</u> <u>lower</u>

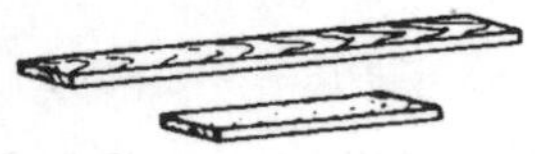

1 Is the lower board ________________ than the other one?
No, it isn't.

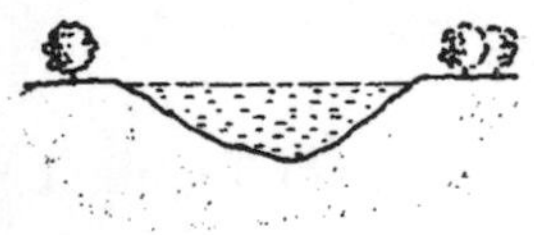

2 Is the middle of a river ________________ than its sides?
Yes, it is.

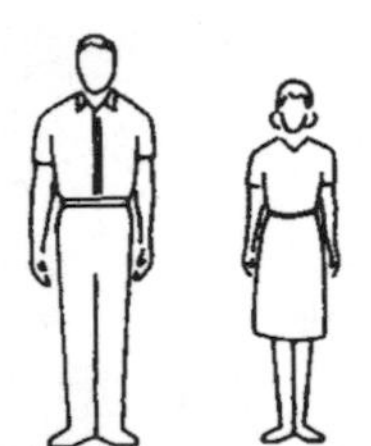

3 Is the woman than ________________ the man?
No, she isn't.

4 Is the 2nd note ________________ than the 1st?
No, it isn't.

Pages **127-132**

<u>gun</u> <u>whistle</u> <u>kettle</u> <u>bucket</u>

<u>sound</u> <u>noise</u>

1 The sound of a ______________ may be very high.

2 It is not good to have a bedroom facing a street in which there is a great amount of ______________ .

3 A ______________ is good for heating water in and a ______________ for taking it from one place to another.

4 The ______________ of music gives pleasure to a great number of us.

5 A ______________ makes a louder noise than a pocket whistle.

This animal is a bat. It is able to go through the air not only in the daytime but at night as well, when there is no light at all. How does it do this and keep clear of trees and houses? We didn't have the answer to this question before 1793. Then a man by the name of Spallanzani got the idea that it was not the bats' eyes but their ears that made them able to go about in the dark. To see if this was true, he took the sense of hearing from a number of bats. When he did this, the bats were not able to keep from going into things. This made it clear that their hearing was the most important sense to bats in motion. But others at that time gave no thought to what Spallanzani said. It took years for others to see that his statements about bats' hearing were true.

Bats make thin, high, short noises, sending sound waves through the air which may be turned back by a tree or a wall or anything in front of them. Sound waves coming back to the bat's ear give the bat knowledge of when something is in front of it and how far away the thing is.

As a bat gets nearer to what is in its way, the sound waves the bat sends out come back to it more quickly. Then the bat makes a change in its direction. This is how it keeps clear of things, on the darkest nights as well as on the brightest days.

1 What sense is very important to a bat?

____

____

2 Does the bat make use of this sense only in the daytime?

____

____

3 What does the bat send out as it goes through the air?

____

____

4 What gives the bat knowledge of when something is in front of it and how far the bat is from it?

____

____

____

<u>myself</u> <u>yourself</u> <u>himself</u> <u>herself</u>

<u>itself</u> <u>ourselves</u> <u>yourselves</u> <u>themselves</u>

1 When the summer is over we are the only family on the island. For nine months we are by ________________.

2 She made all of the dress ________________.

3 Before long, a young bird is able to get its food for ________________.

4 John, are you going by ________________ or are you taking your brother with you?

5 I see________________ in the looking glass every morning.

6 They kept ________________dry by putting on great boots, raincoats, and rainhats.

7 If you and Peter don't do the work now when I am here to do it with you, you will have to do it by ________________ .

8 He seemed to be talking to ________________ , but then I saw there was another person with him.

Pages **130-132**

It was a warm summer day. After working hard in his garden, Mr. Wood was resting in his bedroom when a very loud hammering noise came through an open window. "What on earth is that!" he said. The noise was coming from a bird which was making a hole in a tree not far from the window. "Oh, no!" said Mr. Wood when it became clear to him what the noise was. But he didn't get up at first. Waiting for the bird to get through seemed the only thing to do. However, the hammering kept on. At last Mr. Wood, with his eyes only half open, got up and said to himself, "I'm going to put a stop to that noise!" He went over to the window and put it down very hard, making a noise louder than the hammering of the bird. "Oh, what did I do!" said Mr. Wood, seeing bits of glass and wood on the floor round him. "The window is broken now. And all because of that bird!" After a short time there was again the sound of hammering. Was it the bird? No, this time it was Mr. Wood himself, putting the parts of the window frame together again.

Pages **130-132**

1 What was Mr. Wood doing before he went to the window?

____

____

2 Why didn't he get up at first?

____

____

3 What made him go to the window?

____

____

4 Was he talking to the bird?

____

____

5 When did the window in Mr. Wood's bedroom get broken?

____

____

<u>facing</u> <u>nailing</u> <u>smoking</u> <u>warming</u>
<u>swimming</u> <u>hammering</u> <u>turning</u>

1 A man who is putting two bits of wood together with nails is________________ them together.

2 When he gives blows to the nails with a hammer, he is ________________ them into the wood.

3 Today, most persons say that ________________ has bad effects upon the body.

4 ________________ has a good effect upon the body; it makes the body stronger.

5 When we are ________________the sun, we sometimes have to put dark glasses on or keep our eyes shut.

6 In winter, ________________ ourselves by an open fire gives us a good feeling.

7 When a farmer is plowing, he is ________________ up the earth with a plow.

Put "true" before the statements that are true, "false" before those that are false.

true 1 The man is seated on the bucket.

________ 2 The monkey is at the man's feet.

________ 3 The boy is getting a whistle from the man.

________ 4 There is a cord fixed to the monkey's collar.

________ 5 Water is in the bucket.

________ 6 The monkey's tail is straight.

________ 7 The monkey has his arm round the man's neck.

________ 8 The boy has short trousers on.

Pages **133-136**

In music, the letters A, B, C, D, E, F, and G are the names of notes. In writing, when we put the right letters together, we make words; when we put the right ______________ (music, notes) together, we have ______________ (music, notes). When we put words and music together, we have a ______________ (note, song).

There was a time when we made music by putting one ______________ (note, song) after another, like this:

These ______________ (notes, song) come from a ______________ (notes, song) of about 1400. By 1600, we were making ______________ (music, notes) by putting a number of ______________ (music, notes) together like this:

This ______________ (note, song) has four parts. The two top parts are for women and young boys. The two lower parts are for men.

Some songs have more than four parts. But no ______________ (notes, songs) have the number of parts that ______________ (music, notes) for instruments may have. ______________ (Music, Notes) for instruments may have up to twenty different parts when different instruments are in use together. Here is an instrument which gives us the highest ____________ (notes, songs) of all.

Here is an instrument which gives us the lowest ____________ (notes, music) there are.

1 One way of getting apples from a tree is by giving the tree a ______________ .

2 Not every boy or girl does good ______________ in school.

3 Taking only a quick ________________ at the pages of a book will not give us as much knowledge of it as reading it through will.

4 Taking a ________________ in the sea is a pleasure to some of us on a very warm day.

5 Giving an open door a soft _______________ with the fingers will not put it into motion, but giving it a push will.

<u>worst</u> <u>lowest</u> <u>highest</u> <u>least</u> <u>best</u> <u>most</u>

We three all had the same number of apples this morning. Now at the end of the day, there are no apples here. Mrs. Visconti got a higher price for her apples than Mr. Grassino did for his, and he got a higher price for his than I did for my apples. Mrs. Visconti got the ____________ price and I got the____________ price. A higher price gives you more money. Mrs. Visconti got the ____________money for her apples and I got the ____________ for my apples. And if the higher price is the better price, she got the ____________ price and I got the ____________one.

Pages **140-148**

After every line in these statements is a word. Put the opposite of that word on the line.

1 It is a pleasure____________ (pain) to see something beautiful.

2 We say that the sea is ____________ (smooth) when we see a great number of high waves in it.

3 Whenever there is a great amount of wind and rain, a journey in an airplane may be far from ____________ (rough).

4 It is no pleasure to be with a person who is ____________ (happy) most of the time.

5 A baby's way of saying that he is happy is by ____________ (crying) or giving those round him a smile.

6 When Copernicus said that the earth goes round the sun, some men of the church said his statement was ____________ (true).

7 Monkeys have ____________ (less) brains than goats.

PICTURE A

PICTURE B

Pages **143-149**

Put the letter A before a statement about Picture A, B before a statement about Picture B.

___A___ 1 The man is swimming.

______ 2 The water is a little rough.

______ 3 He is in the water.

______ 4 He has a cat with him.

______ 5 The water is smooth.

______ 6 He is not facing the water.

______ 7 The man is warming himself in the sun.

______ 8 He is at the seaside.

______ 9 He has a dog with him.

______ 10 He is on the sand.

______ 11 He is not at the seaside.

______ 12 He is taking a swim.

______ 13 It is not certain that he is a swimmer.

______ 14 He is not taking a swim.

______ 15 It is certain that he is a swimmer.

Pages **143-149**

Put a line under the words that make a statement true.

1 If A is equal to B and B is equal to C, (then A is equal to C) (then A is not equal to C).

2 If a person goes on with his education, (he does not put a stop to it) (he puts a stop to it).

3 When a person says that something is beautiful, (it is certain that the thing is beautiful) (it is not certain that the thing is beautiful) because there is no measure of the beautiful.

4 If an animal has an attraction for a small boy, (the animal has a desire for the boy) (the boy has a desire for the animal).

5 If a person is facing you, (he has his back to you) (he does not have his back to you).

knowledge sleep talk rate
thoughts wash laugh

1 There is ____________________ that a man will be sent to Mars before 2010.

2 Most boys in school do not keep their _____________ on their work all the time.

3 It is important that we have a certain amount of ____________________ every night.

4 A cat gives itself a _________________ with its tongue.

5 Most of the time the sound of a __________________ is a happy sound.

6 The _________________ at which the earth is turning round is said to be slower than before.

7 It is important that we have __________________ of ourselves and of others.

After hearing a ____________________ (cry, laugh) from her daughter, Mrs. Smith went to see what was ______________ (right, wrong). From the ____________ (doorway, window) of the house, she was able to get a ______________ (happier, clearer) idea of what was going on outside. Her daughter and a little boy were at ______________ (work, play) when the girl had a ______________ (blow, fall) from the boy's cart. When she saw her mother, the girl kept on ____________ (crying, laughing), pointing to the cart at the same time. "So that's how you had the fall," the mother said. "Tom, take the cart ______________ (away, up)," she said to the boy. And then she took her daughter into the house.

1 Dressmakers make clothing of all sorts.

Clothing of all sorts is made ______________________
by dressmakers. ______________________

2 Mary let the cat out of the house.

The cat ______________________

____

3 The government will give money to a great number of schools in the coming year.

Money ______________________

____

4 The sun sends out light in every direction.

Light ______________________

____

5 Sometimes birds take seeds from the earth.

Seeds ______________________

____

6 Tom put the book there.

The books ______________________

____

7 The work which a teacher does has no end.

The work ______________________

____

8 "To be or not to be. That is the question." Hamlet, a person in a play by Shakespeare, said these words.

These words ______________________

____

9 Putting milk in an icebox keeps it good.

Milk ______________________

____

10 Every year a great number of persons see the painting "Mona Lisa."

The painting "Mona Lisa" ______________________

____

____

ANSWERS

The first number indicates the page of the workbook on which the questions appear. The number in parentheses refers to the pages in English Re-start, Book II, which these exercises support.

Page 165 (2-11)

1 She is putting a hairpin in her hair.
2 He is drying his hands.
3 She is putting toothpaste on a toothbrush.
4 They are combing their hair.
5 He is brushing his hair.

Pages 166-167 (2-11)

1 She is in a bedroom.
2 It is between the seat and the chest of drawers.
3 A sock is in her left hand.
4 She sees a hole in the sock.
5 A washcloth is by the basin.
6 They are on the seat.
7 It is between the two windows.
8 It is on the chest of drawers.
9 They are on the bed.
10 They are by the bed.

Page 171 (2-11)

1 going
2 by
3 train, when
4 front
5 journey
6 between
7 before
8 after

Pages 174-175 (2-11)

1 plane
2 bags
3 cloth
4 dry, clean
5 wet, dirty
6 hole
7 basin
8 soap
9 washing, drying
10 brushing, combing
11 pins
12 comb, brush, washcloth

Page 178 (2-15)

1 Wednesday
2 Friday
3 tickets
4 two hundred dollars, office
5 taxi, station
6 Sunday
7 like

Page 179 (2-15)

1 pin
2 house
3 box
4 cloth
5 brush
6 hole
7 pin
8 pot
9 brush
10 box

Page 180 (2-15)

1 bells
2 week, days
3 railroad, rails
4 little
5 cents
6 much
7 engine
8 Monday, Tuesday
9 Wednesday, Thursday
10 Saturday

Page 185 (14-24)

Put the right words in the boxes

Yesterday	Today	Tomorrow
Saturday	Sunday	Monday
Monday	Tuesday	Wednesday
Thursday	Friday	Saturday
Sunday	Monday	Tuesday

Monday			yesterday
Tuesday		yesterday	today
Wednesday	yesterday	today	tomorrow
Thursday	today	tomorrow	
Friday	tomorrow		

Page 181 (2-15)

1 combing
2 brushing
3 washing
4 boiling
5 Waiting

Pages 182-183 (2-15)

1 Shaking
2 friends
3 how
4 Please
5 Let

Page 184 (2-15)

1 open
2 dirty
3 wet
4 thin
5 low
6 bad
7 old
8 long
9 warm
10 front

Pages 186-187 (16-25)

school, board, teaching, learning, school, education, living, teacher, board, writing, paper, pens, letters, words

Page 190 (16-25)

1 town
2 states
3 Cities
4 state
5 city

Page 193 (16-25)

1 out of, steps
2 street
3 letter
4 stamp
5 house
6 post card, friend
7 sends, love
8 post office, hundred

Page 195 (16-25)

1851 South Street
Littleton, Ohio
May 16, 2004

The Town Times
45 High Street
Littleton, Ohio

Dear Sir,

The story in your newspaper on Senator Fillimaster was very good. You are right. Let Senator Fillimaster and his friends in Washington keep their hands off our schools.

Yours truly,
Gordon White

Pages 196-197 (16-25)

1 in an office
2 in a waiting room
3 in a post office
4 in a taxi
5 in a school room
6 in a harbor

Pages 200-201 (16-25)

A 1 It is night in Switzerland.
2 This is Philip.
3 He is in his room writing a story.
4 He will send the story over to his editor before morning.

B 1 It is morning.
2 This is the editor.
3 He is going to his work in the newspaper office.
4 When he gets to the office, he will see Philip's story.

Page 202 (16-25)

1 newspaper
2 look
3 front
4 pages
5 pictures
6 great

Page 203 (16-25)

1 Every tree has roots.
2 ~~Every woman has long hair.~~
3 Every day the sun comes up.
4 ~~Every day you say the same things.~~
5 Every week has seven days in it.
6 ~~Every family has five persons in it~~
7 Every cow is an animal.
8 ~~Every animal is a cow~~

Page 204 (16-25)

1 sun, cloud
2 moon
3 night
4 stars
5 directions

Page 205 (16-25)

Page 206 (16-25)

1 send
2 sending
3 sent

Page 209 (22-25)

1 round
2 west, east
3 a.m., p.m.
4 after
5 before
6 hours
7 hour
8 morning, night

Page 210 (25)

3713 three thousand seven hundred thirteen
3714 three thousand seven hundred fourteen
3716 three thousand seven hundred sixteen
3717 three thousand seven hundred seventeen
3715 three thousand seven hundred fifteen
3718 three thousand seven hundred eighteen

Page 211 (25)

1617 one thousand six hundred seventeen
1619 one thousand six hundred nineteen
1621 one thousand six hundred twenty-one
1623 one thousand six hundred twenty-three

Pages 212-213 (30-39)

1 enough
2 attempt, bent
3 straight
4 better
5 something

Pages 214-215 (31-38)

1 bit
2 wide
3 blade
4 cut
5 wood
6 roof
7 pencil
8 opposite

Pages 216-217 (34-43)

support, hammer, nails, middle, end, down, up, together, bent, straight, broken, strong, enough, stronger, better

Page 218 (35-39)

1 angle 2 right 3 wider 4 cutting

Page 219 (42)

1 It's ready now.
2 No, I don't.
3 No, I wasn't.
4 It's four.
5 No, it isn't.
6 I'm going south for a week.

Pages 220-221 (44-50)

doing, collar, buttonholes, narrow, scissors, needle, thread, button

Page 222 (55-57)

because, months, flowers, March, April, May, spring, stronger, quarter

Page 223 (55-57)

sun, June, July, August, summer, than, warm, half

Page 224 (55-57)

falling, September, October, November, shorter, fall, quarters

Page 225 (55-57)

snow, December, January, February, winter, nights, year

Page 227 (55-71)

map, land, river, Near, sea, island, government, pictures, instruments, distances

Pages 228-229 (57-69)

feet, may, automobiles, miles, about, minutes, quicker, slower, slow, distance, more, sometimes, quick, thick, yards, inches, map, stick, walk, same

Page 230 (59-62)

A 1 oldest
2 older
3 youngest
4 younger

B 1 cleanest
2 cleaner
3 dirtiest
4 dirtier

Page 231 (61-66)

1 thickest, thicker, as, as
2 harder, as, as, hardest, softest

Page 232 (61-66)

1 longest, longer
2 narrowest, widest

Pages 234-235 (61-71)

1 The changes in transport which came between 1800 and 1900 were the steam carriage, the steamship, and the train.
2 They may be making journeys to the moon and other places far from the earth.
3 There are trains, buses, and automobiles for journeys on land. There are steamships for journeys over the water. There are airplanes for journeys through the air.

Pages 236-237 (67-69)

changing, full, dark, brighter, price, land, why, ever

Page 238 (30-71)

1 from
2 to
3 with
4 off
5 from
6 to
7 for
8 in
9 at
10 in

Page 239 (30-71)

1 the girl on the right
2 the man on the right
3 the man on the left
4 the buildings on the right

Page 240 (75-80)

1 spring
2 ball
3 attraction
4 weight
5 fire

Page 241 (75-80)

1 nearer 2 nearest 3 farthest 4 greater

Page 242 (75-80)

sizes, smaller, stick, small, first, middle, last

Page 243 (81-89)

1 writer 2 meter 3 watch 4 statement

Pages 244-245 (81-89)

1 mind
2 hanging
3 square
4 colder
5 motion
6 blows

Page 246 (81-89)

1 science
2 idea
3 one twenty–fifth
4 pull
5 If

Page 247 (81-89)

1 motion
2 rest
3 cause
4 effect
5 false
6 true

Page 248 (81-89)

1 Pounds are a measure of weight.
2 One pound is one-fourth of four pounds.
3 Three times four is twelve.
4 A scale is an instrument for measuring weight.
5 "Light-year" is the measure of distance which light goes in one year.

Page 251 (93-98)

1 discovery
2 only
3 blowing
4 less
5 drops
6 weather
7 worse
8 amount

Pages 252-253 (99-101)

1 smoke, flames, smoke
2 wheels, wheel, wheels
3 cart, bags
4 skirts, short
5 Seeds, worms, birds

Page 254 (99)

1 Why did he give you his watch?
2 I am very happy because he sent me some flowers.
3 My father says that if I keep my room clean, he will give me his old watch.
4 Don't get off the bus before giving me some money.
5 He is writing Mother a letter.
6 Did you give the girl an answer?

Page 255 (80-99)

1 puts
2 takes
3 gets
4 gives
5 comes
6 sends
7 makes
8 goes

Page 256 (99-102)

roll, cotton, sheep, clothing, silkworms, warmer, wool

Page 257 (99-102)

Step one is *cutting the wool off the sheep.*
Step two is *washing and drying the wool.*
Step three is *twisting the wool into threads.*
Step four is *putting the threads on a frame.*
Step five is *making the threads into cloth.*

Page 258 (99-102)

1 twists
2 across
3 warmer
4 silk
5 use

Page 259 (103-107)

1 seems, point, seemed
2 herself, looking glass
3 rays

Pages 260-264 (108-112)

1 Question: What *does he have his foot on?*
Answer: He has his foot on a *spade.*
2 Question: What *is she doing?*
Answer: She is *working* with her needle.
3 Question: *Who makes use of a plow?*
Answer: A *farmer* makes use of a plow.
His work is *farming*. His fields and buildings are his *farm.*
4 Question: Is *the man plowing his field?*
Answer: Yes, the man is *plowing* his *field* to get it ready for putting in seeds.
5 Question: What *does he do for a living?*
Answer: He makes boots and shoes for a living.
He is a *shoemaker.*

6 Question: What does he have in his hands?
Answer: He has his paint in one hand and his paint brush in the other. He is a painter.

7 Question: What is her work?
Answer: Housekeeping is her work. She is a housemaker.

8 Question: What sort of store does he have?
Answer: He has a clothing store. He is a storekeeper.

9 Question: Where does this man go to work every day? Answer: This man goes to work in a bank every day. His work is banking.

10 Question: What is the businessman doing?
Answer: This businessman is keeping accounts for his business.

Pages 265-266 (109-110)

look, bank, account, important, pocket, prices, numbers, addition, cents, check

Page 267 (111-123)

1 as
2 through
3 to
4 with

Page 268 (113-123)

1 a bitter one
2 cake
3 touching
4 salt
5 touching
6 lips

Page 269 (113-123)

1 across
2 in
3 before
4 up
5 in

Page 270 (114-122)

1 We put sugar on food *to give it a sweet taste.*

2 A thing may seem strange *to us if we have no knowledge of it.*

3 Men are able *to make mines which go deep down into the earth.*

4 The two sides of a road seem *to come together in the distance.*

5 An automobile is of great use *to a businessman when his house is far from his work.*

Page 271 (114-124)

1 The grass

2 The garden

3 The sweet smell

4 Her fingernails

5 The glasses

6 The top

Page 272 (114-124)

1 tasting

2 seeing

3 smell

4 reading

5 touch

6 hearing

7 talking

Page 273 (125)

yellow, blue, white, gray, colors, green, red

Pages 274-275 (126-136)

1 No, it isn't.

2 Yes, it is.

3 Yes, he is.

4 No, she isn't.

5 Yes, he is.

6 No, she doesn't.

Page 276 (126-136)

1 longer

2 deeper

3 taller

4 lower

Page 277 (127-132)

1 whistle 2 noise 3 kettle, bucket
4 sound 5 gun

Page 279 (129-149)

1 The sense of hearing is very important to a bat.
2 No, he makes use of it at night as well.
3 It sends out sound waves as it goes through the air.
4 Sound waves coming back to the bat's ear give the bat this knowledge.

Page 280 (130)

1 ourselves
2 herself
3 itself
4 yourself
5 myself
6 themselves
7 yourselves
8 himself

Page 282 (130-132)

1 He was resting in his bedroom.
2 Waiting for the bird to get through seemed the only thing to do.
3 The hammering kept on.
4 No, he was talking to himself.
5 It got broken when Mr. Wood put the window down very hard.

Page 283 (132-149)

1 nailing
2 hammering
3 smoking
4 Swimming
5 facing
6 warming
7 turning

Page 284 (133-135)

1 true 2 false 3 true 4 true
5 false 6 false 7 true 8 true

Pages 285-286 (133-136)

notes, music, song, note
notes, song, music, notes
song, songs, music, music, notes, notes

Page 287 (134-149)

1 shake
2 work
3 look
4 swim
5 touch

Page 288 (135-138)

highest, lowest, most, least, best, worst

Page 289 (140-148)

1 pleasure
2 rough
3 smooth
4 unhappy
5 laughing
6 false
7 more

Page 291 (143-149)

1 A
2 B
3 A
4 B
5 A
6 B
7 B
8 B
9 A
10 B
11 A
12 A
13 B
14 B
15 A

Page 292 (143-149)

1 (then A is equal to C)
2 (he does not put a stop to it)
3 (it is not certain that the thing is beautiful)
4 (the boy has a desire for the animal)
5 (he does not have his back to you)

Page 293 (153)

1 talk
2 thoughts
3 sleep
4 wash
5 laugh
6 rate
7 knowledge

Page 294 (143-154)

cry, wrong, doorway, clearer, play, fall, crying, away

Pages 295-296 (154-156)

1 Clothing of all sorts is made by dressmakers.
2 The cat was let out of the house by Mary.
3 Money will be given to a great number of schools in the coming year.
4 Light is sent out in every direction by the sun.
5 Seeds are sometimes taken from the earth by birds.
6 The books were put there by Tom.
7 The work done by a teacher has no end.
8 These words were said by Hamlet, a person in a play by Shakespeare.
9 Milk is kept good by putting it in an icebox.
10 The painting "Mona Lisa" is seen by a great number of persons every year.

INDEX

The number after each word indicates the page of the text on which the word first occurs.
This index includes words of *English Re-start*
(Only words taught in this book carry page numbers.)